The Conflict-Positive Organization

Stimulate Diversity and Create Unity

Dean Tjosvold

Simon Fraser University

 ADDISON-WESLEY PUBLISHING COMPANY
*Reading, Massachusetts • Menlo Park, California • New York
Don Mills, Ontario • Wokingham, England • Amsterdam • Bonn
Sydney • Singapore • Tokyo • Madrid • San Juan*

*To Mary Tjosvold who, through love and
conflict, has built businesses and developed
people*

Library of Congress Cataloging-in-Publication Data

Tjosvold, Dean.
   The conflict-positive organization: stimulate diversity and create
unity/Dean Tjosvold.
      p.   cm.
   Includes bibliographical references.
   ISBN 0-201-51485-0
   1. Conflict management.   I. Title.
HD42.T58 1991
658.4—dc20
                                                        90-296
                                                        CIP

This book is in the Addison-Wesley Series on Organization Development.
Editors: Edgar H. Schein, Richard Beckhard

Reprinted with corrections, July 1992.

3 4 5 6 7 8 9 10 BA 9594

Other Titles in the Organization Development Series

Parallel Learning Structures: Increasing Innovation in Bureaucracies
Gervase R. Bushe and A.B. Shani

1991 (52427)

Parallel learning structures are technostructural interventions that promote system-wide change in bureaucracies while retaining the advantages of bureaucratic design. This text serves as a resource of models and theories built around five cases of parallel learning structures that can help those who create and maintain them be more effective and successful. For those new to parallel learning structures, the text provides practical advice as to when and how to use them.

The Strategic Management Process: Integrating the OD Perspective
David Hitchin and Walter Ross

1991 (52429)

Written for CEOs, general managers, OD professionals, and strategic-planning specialists, this text integrates the OD perspective into the strategic-management process. This approach begins with the authors' belief that building and sustaining a healthy, high-performance organization is dependent upon the fact that people are the key to organizational success, and that their management is critical to successful strategic planning and execution. The authors' philosophy and suggestions for the strategic management of both profit and nonprofit organizations are presented.

Managing in the New Team Environment: Skills, Tools, and Methods
Larry Hirschhorn

1991 (52503)

This text is designed to help manage the tensions and complexities that arise for managers seeking to guide employees in a team environment. Based on an interactive video course developed at IBM, the text takes managers step by step through the process of building a team and authorizing it to act while they learn to step back and delegate. Specific issues addressed are how to give a team structure, how to facilitate its basic processes, and how to acknowledge differences in relationships among team members and between the manager and individual team members.

Change by Design
Robert R. Blake, Jane Srygley Mouton, and Anne Adams McCanse

1989 (50748)

This book develops a systematic approach to organization development and provides readers with rich illustrations of coherent planned change. The book involves testing, examining, revising, and strengthening conceptual foundations in order to create sharper corporate focus and increased predictability of successful organization development.

Organization Development in Health Care
R. Wayne Boss

1989 (18364)

This is the first book to discuss the intricacies of the health care industry. The book explains the impact of OD in creating healthy and viable organizations in the health care sector. Through unique and innovative techniques, hospitals are able to reduce nursing turnover, thereby resolving the nursing shortage problem. The text also addresses how OD can improve such bottom-line variables as cash flow and net profits.

Self-Designing Organizations: Learning How to Create High Performance
Susan Albers Mohrman and Thomas G. Cummings

1989 (14603)

This book looks beyond traditional approaches to organizational transition, offering a strategy for developing organizations that enables them to learn not only how to adjust to the dynamic environment in which they exist, but also how to achieve a higher level of performance. This strategy assumes that change is a learning process: the goal is continually refined as organizational members learn how to function more effectively and respond to dynamic conditions in their environment.

Power and Organization Development: Mobilizing Power to Implement Change
Larry E. Greiner and Virginia E. Schein

1988 (12185)

This book forges an important collaborative approach between two opposing and often contradictory approaches to management: OD practitioners who espouse a "more humane" workplace without understanding the political realities of getting things done, and practicing managers who feel comfortable with power but overlook the role of human potential in contributing to positive results.

Designing Organizations for High Performance
David P. Hanna

1988 (12693)

This book is the first to give insight into the actual processes you can use to translate organizational concepts into bottom-line improvements. Hanna's "how-to" approach shows not only the successful methods of intervention, but also the plans behind them and the corresponding results.

Process Consultation, Volume 1: Its Role in Organization Development, Second Edition
Edgar H. Schein

1988 (06736)

How can a situation be influenced in the workplace without the direct use of power or formal authority? This book presents the core theoretical foundations and basic prescriptions for effective management.

Organizational Transitions: Managing Complex Change, Second Edition
Richard Beckhard and Reuben T. Harris

1987 (10887)

This book discusses the choices involved in developing a management system appropriate to the "transition state." It also discusses commitment to change, organizational culture, and increasing and maintaining productivity, creativity, and innovation.

Organization Development: A Normative View
W. Warner Burke

1987 (10697)

This book concisely describes and defines the theories and practices of organization development and also looks at organization development as change in an organization's culture. It is a useful guide to the field of organization development and is invaluable to managers, executives, practitioners, and anyone desiring an excellent overview of this multifaceted field.

Team Building: Issues and Alternatives, Second Edition
William G. Dyer

1987 (18037)

Through the use of the techniques and procedures described in this book, managers and consultants can effectively prepare, apply, and follow up on the human processes affecting the productive functioning of teams.

The Technology Connection: Strategy and Change in the Information Age
Marc S. Gerstein

1987 (12188)

This is a book that guides managers and consultants through crucial decisions about the use of technology for increasing effectiveness and competitive advantage. It provides a useful way to think about the relationship between information technology, business strategy, and the process of change in organizations.

Stream Analysis: A Powerful Way to Diagnose and Manage Organizational Change
Jerry I. Porras

1987 (05693)

Drawing on a conceptual framework that helps the reader to better understand organizations, this book shows how to diagnose failings in organizational functioning and how to plan a comprehensive set of actions needed to change the organization into a more effective system.

Process Consultation, Volume II: Lessons for Managers and Consultants
Edgar H. Schein

1987 (06744)

This book shows the viability of the process consultation model for working with human systems. Like Schein's first volume on process consultation, the second volume focuses on the moment-to-moment behavior of the manager or consultant rather than on the design of the OD program.

Managing Conflict: Interpersonal Dialogue and Third-Party Roles, Second Edition
Richard E. Walton

1987 (08859)

This book shows how to implement a dialogue approach to conflict management. It presents a framework for diagnosing recurring conflicts and suggests several basic options for controlling or resolving them.

Pay and Organization Development
Edward E. Lawler

1981 (03990)

This book examines the important role that reward systems play in organization development efforts. By combining examples and specific recommendations with conceptual material, it organizes the various topics and puts them into a total systems perspective. Specific pay approaches such as gainsharing, skill-based pay, and flexible benefits are discussed and their impact on productivity and the quality of work life is analyzed.

Work Redesign
J. Richard Hackman and Greg R. Oldham

1980 (02779)

This book is a comprehensive, clearly written study of work design as a strategy for personal and organizational change. Linking theory and practical technologies, it develops traditional and alternative approaches to work design that can benefit both individuals and organizations.

Organizational Dynamics: Diagnosis and Intervention
John P. Kotter

1978 (03890)

This book offers managers and OD specialists a powerful method of diagnosing organizational problems and of deciding when, where, and how to use (or not use) the diverse and growing number of organizational improvement tools that are available today. Comprehensive and fully integrated, the book includes many different concepts, research findings, and competing philosophies and provides specific examples of how to use the information to improve organizational functioning.

Career Dynamics: Matching Individual and Organizational Needs
Edgar H. Schein

1978 (06834)

This book studies the complexities of career development from both an individual and an organizational perspective. Changing needs throughout the adult life cycle, interaction of work and family, and integration of individual and organizational goals through human resource planning and development are all thoroughly explored.

Matrix
Stanley M. Davis and Paul Lawrence

1977 (01115)

This book defines and describes the matrix organization, a significant departure from the traditional "one man-one boss" management system. The author notes that the tension between the need for independence (fostering innovation) and order (fostering efficiency) drives organizations to consider a matrix system. Among the issues addressed are reasons for using a matrix, methods for establishing one, the impact of the system on individuals, its hazards, and what types of organizations can use a matrix system.

Feedback and Organization Development: Using Data-Based Methods
David A. Nadler

1977 (05006)

This book addresses the use of data as a tool for organizational change. It attempts to bring together some of what is known from experience and research and to translate that knowledge into useful insights for those who are thinking about using data-based methods in organizations. The broad approach of the text is to treat a whole range of questions and issues considering the various uses of data as an organizational change tool.

Designing Complex Organizations
Jay Galbraith
1973 (02559)
This book attempts to present an analytical framework of the design of organizations, particularly of types of organizations that apply lateral decision processes or matrix forms. These forms have become pervasive in all types of organizations, yet there is little systematic public knowledge about them. This book helps fill this gap.

Organization Development: Strategies and Models
Richard Beckhard
1969 (00448)
This book is written for managers, specialists, and students of management who are concerned with the planning of organization development programs to resolve the dilemmas brought about by a rapidly changing environment. Practiced teams of interdependent people must spend real time improving their methods of working, decision making, and communicating, and a planned, managed change is the first step toward effecting and maintaining these improvements.

Organization Development: Its Nature, Origins, and Prospects
Warren G. Bennis
1969 (00523)
This primer on OD is written with an eye toward the people in organizations who are interested in learning more about this educational strategy as well as for those practitioners and students of OD who may want a basic statement both to learn from and to argue with. The author treats the subject with a minimum of academic jargon and a maximum of concrete examples drawn from his own and others' experience.

Developing Organizations: Diagnosis and Action
Paul R. Lawrence and Jay W. Lorsch
1969 (04204)
This book is a personal statement of the authors' evolving experience, through research and consulting, in the work of developing organizations. The text presents the authors' overview of organization development, then proceeds to examine issues at each of three critical interfaces: the organization-environment interface, the group-group interface, and the individual-organization interface, including brief examples of work on each. The text concludes by pulling the themes together in a set of conclusions about organizational development issues as they present themselves to practicing managers.

About the Author

Dean Tjosvold (Ph.D., University of Minnesota) is Professor, Faculty of Business Administration, Simon Fraser University, in the Vancouver suburb of Burnaby, British Columbia. He has published over 100 articles on managing conflict, cooperation and competition, decision making, power, and other management issues. With his sister, Mary Tjosvold, he has written two books for health care professionals. With David W. Johnson, he edited *Productive Conflict Management: Perspectives for Organizations* (Minneapolis: Team Media, 1989). He authored *Working Together to Get Things Done: Managing for Organizational Productivity* (Boston: Lexington Books, 1986) and recently published *Managing Conflict: The Key to Making an Organization Work* (Minneapolis: Team Media, 1989). He has just completed *Team Organization: An Enduring Competitive Advantage* (Wiley) as part of the Industrial and Organizational Psychology Series. He consults on conflict management and related issues and is a partner in several health care businesses in Minnesota.

Foreword

The Addison-Wesley Series on Organization Development originated in the late 1960s when a number of us recognized that the rapidly growing field of "OD" was not well understood or well defined. We also recognized that there was no one OD philosophy, and hence one could not at that time write a textbook on the theory and practice of OD, but one could make clear what various practitioners were doing under that label. So the original six books launched what has since become a continuing enterprise, the essence of which was to allow different authors to speak for themselves instead of trying to summarize under one umbrella what was obviously a rapidly growing and highly diverse field.

By the early 1980s the series included nineteen titles. OD was growing by leaps and bounds, and it was expanding into all kinds of organizational areas and technologies of intervention. By this time, many textbooks existed as well that tried to capture the core concepts of the field, but we felt that diversity and innovation were still the more salient aspects of OD.

Now as we move into the 1990s our series includes twenty-seven titles, and we are beginning to see some real convergence in the underlying assumptions of OD. As we observe how different professionals working in different kinds of organizations and occupational communities make their case, we see we are still far from having a single "theory" of organization development. Yet, a set of common assumptions is surfacing. We are beginning to see patterns in what works and what does not work, and we are becoming more articulate about these patterns. We are also seeing the field connecting to broader themes in the organizational sciences, and new theories and theories of practice are being presented in such areas as conflict resolution, group dynamics, and the process of change in relationship to culture. The new titles in the series address current themes directly: Tjosvold's *The Conflict-Positive Organization,* for example, connects to a whole research tradition on the dynamics of collaboration, competition, and conflict; Hirschhorn's *Managing in the New Team Environment* contains important links to psychoanalytic group theory; Bushe and Shani's *Parallel Learning Structures* presents a seminal theory of large-scale organization change based on the institution of parallel systems as change agents; and Hitchin and Ross's *The Strategic Management Process* looks at the connection between strategic planning theory and practice and implementation through OD interventions.

As editors we have not dictated these connections, nor have we asked authors to work on higher-order concepts and theories. It is just happening, and it is a welcome turn of events. Perhaps it is an indication that OD may be reaching a period of consolidation and integration. We hope that we can contribute to this trend with future volumes.

Cambridge, Massachusetts   Richard H. Beckhard
New York, New York   Edgar H. Schein

Preface

The Conflict-Positive Organization is about how managers and employees can use conflict to forge a spirited, united company. It is about how you and your colleagues can take charge of your conflicts to promote the innovation and productivity of your company and the competence and well-being of its people. It shows how positive conflict is vital if a company is to achieve continuous improvement and competitive advantage.

Wars, strikes, and protests capture newspaper headlines, but everyone who works in an organization argues, doubts, and ventilates. Unfortunately, far too often conflict is so misunderstood and mismanaged that it disrupts the communication and teamwork necessary for organizational effectiveness. People try to check their ideas and feelings until they become so frustrated that they explode in anger or walk away in despair. They blame conflict and give it the power to destroy.

This book describes the potential of positive conflict. Research studies document that conflict can be a powerful force for finding a common ground, solving problems, and strengthening morale and relationships. Well-managed conflict invigorates and empowers teams and organizations. Without a full airing of different points of views, decisions can be disastrous, common tasks meaningless, and relationships shallow. Life without conflict is both unproductive and dull.

Sensing its potential, innovative managers have begun to create organizations that promote positive conflict. Managers want a more open, organic organization that discards formalism and fosters the ongoing communication and exchange needed for hustle and swift action to compete in a turbulent, fast-changing environment.[*] They are establishing strong corporate cultures and visions, using multiskilled work groups and multiperspective project teams within a flatter organizational structure, and striving for an ethical business with a social conscience. They are seeking competitive advantages through synergy between marketing and production, employee involvement, and labor-management cooperation.

Positive conflict is needed to make these new forms of organizations work. New intentions and slogans must be backed up with consistent action. Managers lose credibility if they ask employees to participate and get involved, and then bristle at their ideas for change. Work groups and project teams lose their effectiveness if they suppress different points of view.

The Possibilities of Positive Conflict

This book presents an elegant framework for developing and managing positive conflict in the workplace. People who value diverse points of view and experiences, seek "win-win" solutions good for themselves and their colleagues, empower each other to feel confident and skillful, and take stock and develop their abilities turn the disaster of escalating conflict into positive conflict.

I know that managing conflict is not easy and that traditional ideas and approaches to working and organizing interfere with it. It has taken me twenty years to build the research, theory, and practical experience needed to write this book. My research has illuminated basic processes in conflict and the conditions that make it positive. Recent studies have identified when and how these positive-conflict dynamics help leaders and employees, customers and sales representatives, accounting and line managers, and others innovate, improve customer service, and manage costs. Many other researchers have also worked hard to understand conflict and develop the knowledge needed to manage it.

---

[*] T. J. Peters, *Thriving on Chaos: Handbook for a Management Revolution* (New York: Knopf, 1988).

I also know that managing conflict is possible. Executives, managers, and workers in many kinds of organizations have described to us how they have managed specific conflicts effectively and creatively. People with whom I have consulted are most intrigued by the idea of positive conflict. They confront conflict repeatedly and want the more straightforward, effective ways of working that positive conflict offers. Few people do not want to manage conflicts more openly and constructively.

Wanting to manage conflict, however, is insufficient; managers and employees must believe that positive conflict is possible and that they can do it. People need an intellectual roadmap and accompanying strategies and procedures to make conflict constructive. They must also believe that their coworkers and managers are committed to dealing with conflicts more successfully. One person cannot manage conflict alone. A conflict-positive organizational culture enables managers and employees to use their differences to promote their common mission.

This book describes ideas and procedures for making conflict positive and suggests how people working together can develop an organization that puts positive conflict to work. It provides guides for using conflict to make decisions, negotiate a common ground, create a vision, and serve customers. It also includes discussions on threats to positive conflict and the pitfalls you want to avoid.

Telling the Story of Positive Conflict

Conflict is a window to the drama of organizational life. Conflict is rooted in the intricacies of personalities and relationships; it is not about abstract forces or generalities. It seems appropriate to use dialogue and characters to describe positive conflict.* The case of Lee Cement is based on an actual company and real people; however, the case should be considered a docudrama rather than a journalistic report of events. The case illustrates how positive conflict can be introduced and used to strengthen a company.

Not every company will be receptive to positive conflict as Lee was. Becoming conflict-positive requires the joint effort of manage-

---

* D. Tjosvold, *Managing Conflict: The Key to Making Your Organization Work* (Minneapolis: Team Media, 1989).

ment, supervisors, and workers. If one group refuses to get involved, the program is unlikely to succeed. At times, people are too competitive and hostile to learn how to deal with conflict. Alternatively, managers and employees may be so committed to avoiding conflict that the notion of making conflict public and productive is just too radical.

While a crisis can make evident the need to deal with conflicts before problems become emergencies, a company in the midst of a crisis that threatens its survival, while having high need to become more conflict-positive, probably lacks the openness and the time required to reflect upon its approaches and develop new ones. A company is more prepared to become conflict-positive when all of its people understand the need to deal with conflict and have some degree of latitude, openness, and trust in the first place.

A conflict-positive approach is not a priority for every organization. In some companies, people have learned to conflict adequately and are unlikely to confront more difficult conflicts in the future. Traditional hierarchical organizations facilitate regular, ordered behavior, which is useful for operating effectively in a stable environment, and they minimize time-consuming, costly communication and conflict managing. A company that must respond to turbulent changes within and outside of the company, however, can benefit from a conflict-positive program.

The Book's Structure

The book is divided into five Parts. Part I, Confronting Conflict, describes an organizational conflict at Lee Cement that illustrates the major themes—that conflict is pervasive, and avoiding and failing to managing it can be very costly. Chapter 2 discusses the conflict-positive model.

Part II, Coping with a Conflict, shows how the conflict-positive model can be used to deal with a conflict that has already escalated and disrupted work relationships. In Chapter 3, a consultant prepares one group at Lee for dealing with conflict. Chapter 4 begins the process of direct discussion between groups.

In Part III, Positive Conflict at Work, positive conflict is shown to contribute to organizational success and displays its intellectual and emotional sides. Chapter 5 outlines how opposing views can be structured to enhance decision making. In Chapter 6, the conflict-positive model guides negotiating and changing frustrating procedures and ways of working. Chapter 7 indicates how anger can be managed to promote morale and unleash energy.

Part IV, A Positive-Conflict Culture and Structure, explores how managers and employees can create a climate and opportunities to put positive conflict to work and avoid escalating destructive conflict. Chapter 8 argues that positive conflict contributes significantly to organizational unity. Chapter 9 describes how well-structured teams provide the tasks, rewards, mandate, and opportunities for managing conflict positively. Positive conflict is an important way that an organization strives to be fair and ethical and shows it deserves high commitment (Chapter 10).

Part V, Conflict-Positive Organization Development, relates the book's themes and ideas to organizational change issues. The conflict-positive model provides a common aspiration and suggests strategies employees, leaders, and change agents can use to be effective (Chapter 11). Chapter 12 summarizes the argument that positive conflict is a vital, underlying competitive advantage because, through it, companies continue to develop new products, improve quality, reduce costs, and deliver value to customers.

Acknowledgments

I am grateful to many people for their assistance and support in writing this book. Chris Argyris, Bob Baron, Max Bazerman, Robert Blake, Peter Carnevale, Rick Cosier, Barbara Gray, Len Greenhalgh, Irving Janis, Boris Kabonoff, Roy Lewicki, Keith Murnigham, Maggie Neal, Dean Pruitt, Linda Putman, Afzal Rahim, Blair Sheppard, Ken Thomas, Evert van de Vliert, Jim Wall, and many other capable researchers have helped us understand the fundamental role of conflict in organizations and have identified how we can manage conflict constructively. I am proud to be in the research tradition of David W. Johnson, Morton Deutsch, and Kurt Lewin.

I thank the many managers and employees with whom I have worked over the years. Their ideas, experiences, and conflicts have stimulated my thinking and broadened my perspective. Mary Tjosvold and Margaret Tjosvold demonstrated many successful ways to manage conflict. Ed Schein, Dick Beckhard, Mark Wexler, Blair Sheppard, and Peter Vail helped developed the approach to presenting the material. Lu Fernandes suggested a number of useful additions and contributed to the summaries. I also thank Jenny Tjosvold for her thorough research and critique of my writing. She, along with our sons and daughters, provided a rich environment for working.

Vancouver, British Columbia   D. T.

Contents

Introduction

Have you learned lessons only of those who admired you, and were tender with you, and stood aside for you? Have you not learned great lessons from those who braced themselves against you, and disputed the passage with you?
Walt Whitman

He that wrestles with us strengthens our nerves, and sharpens our skill. Our antagonist is our helper.
Edmund Burke, *Reflection of the Revolution in France*

When two [people] in business always agree, one of them is unnecessary.
William Wrigley, Jr.

Conflict is doubled-edged. It evokes images of fighting, hostility, and painful divisiveness, but also of people discussing issues deeply and honestly and creating a common ground. Hard-charging people run over others for self-aggrandizement, but also get things done and create wealth. Conflict provokes fears of chaotic revolutions and the excitement of revolutionary innovation. Will conflict transform or destroy our organizations?

Conflict is sharp as well as double-edged. We debate issues of what is just, right, and wrong; we argue about what our families and organizations should do. We protect our interests, yet reach out to understand and accommodate the needs and hopes of others. With such heavy stakes, we are often excited and anxious, and may be outraged or despairing.

Conflict tests us and our organizations. Dealing effectively with conflict requires intellectual understanding, honest self-examination, reaching out to others, and mature management of feelings. When we use our conflicts rather than fear and avoid them, we invigorate our organizations and ourselves.

The Need to Manage

A common assumption is that conflict is so destructive that the goal of good management is to minimize conflict. This assumption is idealistic and harmful. People are often in conflict, but get upset and perplexed just because they are. They quickly blame each other, but blaming does not get a company closer to achieving its goals.

Managers and workers conflict daily. How can they improve product quality and reduce costs, and who is responsible? Are the probable future returns worth the risks and costs of developing a new product? Should the company grow by expansion or acquisition? Are salaries equitable and performance evaluations accurate? Much conflict involves styles and relationships. The boss is too autocratic, the subordinate rocks the boat, the partner is too passive, the climate is closed and up-tight, management and union distrust each other.

Conflicts over issues often escalate to conflicts over relationships. An employee becomes angry not just because her boss disagrees with her about how to improve safety, but because he is arrogant and closed-minded in discussing it. *Many conflicts in and out of organizations are over how people handle conflict.* These relationship conflicts are particularly hard to manage because they require the protagonists to deal directly with emotions and personal styles.

Conflicts, when appropriately managed, add substantial value to organizations. Conflict is the medium by which problems are recognized and solved. Employees who discuss conflict disclose information, challenge assumptions, dig into issues, and, as a consequence, make successful decisions. Conflict is needed because diverse opinions and information are mandatory to solve problems and get things done in organizations.

Dealing with the conflict improves quality, reduces costs, upgrades leadership, stimulates brainstorming and teamwork, and institutes new procedures to improve company operations. Conflict is not the problem; conflict is part of the solution.

Conflicts can of course be highly costly. Uncontrolled conflict rips apart relationships, sabotages collective work, and devastates people. Wars, strife, strikes, and divorces confirm that escalated conflict destroys. Ill-managed conflicts cost money and hurt the bottom line. Managers and employees use their time brooding and fighting rather than working; projects are delayed; materials are wasted.[1]

Understanding Conflict

• Conflict pervades organizational life.

• Poorly managed conflicts cost a great deal.

• No one wins when conflict escalates.

• It takes two to get tangled into conflict; it takes two to untangle.

• Conflict is not the problem; it is part of the solution.

• Diversity of opinion and information are mandatory to solve problems.

• Conflict reconciles opposing tensions and directions into workable solutions.

Conflict's Benefits

• **Problem awareness.** Discussing frustrations identifies poor quality, excessive costs, injustices, and other barriers to effectiveness.

- **Organizational change.** Conflict creates incentives to challenge and change outmoded procedures, assignments, and structures.

- **Improved solutions.** Debating opposing views digs into issues, searches for information and insight, and integrates ideas to create solutions responsive to several perspectives.

- **Morale.** Employees release their tensions through discussion and problem solving. They feel confident that they have faced difficulties together, and their relationships are strong and open.

- **Personal development.** Managers and employees learn how their style affects others and learn the competencies they need to develop.

- **Self- and other awareness.** People learn what makes themselves and others irritated and angry and what is important to them. Knowing what people are willing to fight about keeps them in touch.

- **Psychological maturity.** People take the perspectives of others and become less egocentric. They feel confident and powerful they can cope with difficulties by dealing directly with them.

- **Fun.** Employees enjoy the stimulation, arousal, and involvement of conflict, and it can be a welcome break from an easy-going pace. Conflict invites people to examine and appreciate the intricacies of their relationships.

Poorly managed conflicts pose great hazards because they disrupt the ability to solve problems, including the ability to deal with conflict. In escalating conflict, people communicate in closed, impoverished, and biased ways. As a result they are unable to discuss the underlying issues and develop solutions to end the conflict.

Ill-managed conflict attacks joint problem solving and, thereby, the very essence of an effective organization.

The Problem Is Avoidance

The idea that conflict is destructive and causes misery is so self-evident that it is seldom debated. Employees fight about many issues, but the wisdom of avoiding conflict is too often not one of them. However, it is the failure to use conflict that causes the distress and low productivity associated with escalating conflict. *Conflict avoidance and the failure to develop an organization equipped to manage it, not conflict itself, disrupt.* Open, skillful discussion is needed to turn differences into synergistic gains rather than squabbling losses.

Yet people work hard to avoid conflict. While they complain bitterly and gossip to their friends, they smile and nod in agreement with their antagonist. They hope issues and hostilities will work themselves out. But when conflict continues and escalates, people are surprised, agitated, and angry, and feel controlled by the conflict rather than in charge of it. Avoiding conflict does not make problems disappear, but allows them to linger and fester, and then emerge in more divisive ways.

Managers and workers have many reasons and excuses for avoiding direct confrontation. They assume that others are getting what they want and are unmotivated to work on the conflict. The antagonists like being angry, and are in control and winning the conflict. Alternatively, they believe that people, including themselves, are too weak and vulnerable to confront a conflict directly. Nor has the organization provided the forums and procedures to deal with conflict. The only viable option is to get out of each other's way as much as possible.

The great irony of conflict is that people and organizations who are highly committed to avoiding escalating, destructive conflict often get themselves into the most painful conflict. They want close, affirming relationships, but confuse ends with means. They assume the way to strong relationships is through harmony and avoiding conflict. However, avoiding conflict makes it very difficult to deal realistically with the inevitable frustrations and difficulties. The result is the potential for escalating, threatening conflict.

To work in an organization is to be in conflict. Even if we could avoid conflict, which we cannot, we do not want to. Conflict revitalizes and rejuvenates. There is no escape from conflict; there is no realistic alternative to managing conflict.

An Ancient Practice with Contemporary Pressures

The need to manage conflict is as old as group life. Throughout history, people, including our ancestors in hunting and gathering societies, developed ways to manage conflict. Every child is continually learning to cope with conflicts with parents, siblings, peers, and teachers. Parents and educators socialize children to relate to other people and manage their conflicts. Every employee must deal with conflict with colleagues and bosses.

Employees and managers have learned important and valuable skills in managing conflict. In our interviews, hundreds of executives, middle managers, workers, customer representatives, professionals, and technicians have described productive, creative ways they have dealt with conflict. However, these same people have also told us of conflicts they have mishandled that cost them and their companies dearly.

The problem is not that people cannot manage any conflict, but that they have many difficult conflicts. Today, organizations require people to manage conflicts in situations in which humankind has little experience.

Managers and employees are asked to resolve conflicts with people trained to think much differently. Production workers and computer specialists are expected to work together to produce cement. Surgeons, anesthetists, laser specialists, and nurses must coordinate to destroy cancerous cells; they must in turn work with administrators, accountants, investors, and government agencies in their cancer clinic.

Contemporary employees are expected to manage many conflicts with people they barely know, and may not even see. A team is expected to create a new product in six months, and then disband. Computer specialists in different divisions and parts of the country are asked to develop the company's information system.

The intensely competitive marketplace adds urgency to conflict managing. Companies are trying to operate lean to maintain profits and satisfy shareholders, and at the same time remain nimble to respond to and exploit market changes. Executives want the company's divisions to coordinate work to deliver new products quickly and cost effectively. Companies are joining forces in joint ventures to pool research capabilities, expand markets, and use new technology.

Globalization of the economy and intensifying world interdependence demand new conflict-management practices. A stock market crash in New York quickly impacts the world markets. A nuclear explosion in the Soviet Union moves Europeans to give assistance and to protect themselves. The investment plans of a Japanese manufacturer alter the plans of families in a small town in Ohio. Japanese producers of computer parts, Singaporean assemblers, and European marketers must deal with conflicts over telephone, fax, and computer lines.

Managing conflict with unknown people with different language and cultural and national backgrounds, who belong to a another division or even company, trained in a narrow specialization under pressure for speed and efficiency tests our capabilities. Misunderstandings and misconceptions very much interfere with our ability to cope with these challenging, emerging conflicts. And the costs of failing to deal with them can be high, even deadly. People need theory tested and developed through research to clarify confusions and provide a framework for action.

The Airplane Cockpit: A New Setting for Conflict Managing

Conflict is needed to maintain the margin of safety of an airplane. More than two-thirds of all air accidents result from "pilot error," which usually is a failure of crew members to use their information expeditiously to cope with safety hazards. Traditionally, airplanes were managed by a highly centralized chain of command and rigid role prescriptions. The captain had supreme authority and responsibility for the airplane, and each flight-crew member was trained and tested on fulfilling specific duties. Today it is recognized that this approach can be disastrous because it may make officers reluctant to disagree with pilots, and such delays have been found to contribute significantly to crashes.[2] Flight-crew members are being trained to develop a team that together deals with threats to airplane safety.[3]

Pilots, first and second officers, and flight attendants discussed specific cases of when safety was and was not restored expeditiously.[4] The cases confirm the positive role of conflict for maintaining safety in the sky and the dangers of avoiding conflict or discussing it unskillfully.

For example, a 747 was in a very vulnerable position when the first officer hesitated and then used diplomacy to inform the pilot that they were not on the proper flight path and had not been given clearance to land. Only at 800 feet did the officer begin yelling instructions that, fortunately, the captain obeyed. Conflict was also very useful when after an engine failed, crew members felt free to propose a variety of alternatives. They ruled out returning to their point of departure because of poor weather, and decided on a delay in dumping the fuel and selected a new destination. They all felt confident the best decision had been made.

The statistical analysis indicates that conflict was very important for dealing with threats in these cases. Constructive conflict explained from 21 to 74 percent of the variance on the measures of restoring safety, using safe procedures, efficiently dealing with the problem, and gaining confidence in working with other flight-crew members. Pilots, officers, and flight attendants, as they work as a team, need to manage their conflicts openly and efficiently to maintain the margin of safety in the sky.

The Conflict-Positive Framework

Nothing is so useful as a good theory.
> Kurt Lewin, pioneer of contemporary social psychology and action research.

Motivation is often blamed for destructive conflict. People are meanspirited and nasty; they don't really want to deal with conflict directly. However, people usually want honest relationships in which problems are addressed forthrightly. The problem is knowing how.

And as conflict requires joint work, both sides must together understand how they can manage their conflict.

This book's theoretical framework clarifies assumptions and strategies to help people manage their conflict. The ideas are useful for coping with conflicts that have already escalated and disrupted relationships and communication. The framework also shows how to put conflict to work to involve managers and employees to become a united, competent force. Positive conflict helps develop a synergistic company able to grapple with threats and create solutions.

Positive conflict has four reinforcing components. (1) People *value their diversity* and appreciate the inevitability of conflict. They look for opportunities to voice their opposing views and discuss frustrations and work to make their relationships productive. (2) People *seek mutual benefit*. They understand that they have mutual interests and seek common ground. They are all committed to pursuing their shared vision and creating a work environment that is fair and facilitating for all. (3) They feel *empowered*. They are not overwhelmed by conflict, but feel in charge of it. They are confident they and their colleagues have the mandate, opportunities, and skills to manage conflict. (4) They regularly *take stock and reflect* on their conflict handling. They realize that becoming conflict-positive requires continuous experimenting, feedback, and improvement.

Successfully moving through these phases strengthens future conflict managing. A reinforcing, beneficial cycle of managing conflict is created in which people cherish their diversities, feel positively dependent upon each other, appreciate each other's abilities and build upon them, and celebrate their joint success and set new improvement goals. In this way, they become more able and willing to confront their differences, emphasize their cooperative interests, and integrate their viewpoints.

Positive conflict is not the only viable way to handle conflicts.[5] At times, competitive conflict is appropriate: owners sue a partner for fraud and breach of fiduciary responsibility; companies battle over the rights to a new product; managers vie for one promotion. Avoiding and smoothing over can also be useful: some conflicts are not worth the bother. Avoiding conflict is also appropriate when a lack of trust and skill make it unlikely that conflict will be constructive.

The argument here is that *positive conflict should be the dominant, not the only, approach to managing conflict* because it maximizes benefits and minimizes costs in most organizational

situations. More generally, *positive conflict should be the overall
context in which people work together, although on occasion they
avoid it and try to win.* Managers fighting over a promotion still
recognize that they need to work together on a number of issues or
risk damaging the company and their own reputations. They try to
limit and control their competition by emphasizing their overall
cooperative interests.

The Conflict-Negative Organization

The underlying assumption is that conflict is negative and
potentially very harmful and that it therefore must be mini-
mized or quickly stopped.

- Tasks are assigned to individuals; individuals are the basic
  building blocks of the organization.

- There are written rules and procedures.

- Impersonal relationships are encouraged in order to minimize the effects of emotions.

- Managerial leaders are expected to make decisions and
  solve problems decisively.

The Conflict-Positive Organization

The underlying assumption is that conflict is potentially very
productive, but must be used skillfully to realize this potential.

- Tasks are assigned to groups; groups are the basic building
  blocks of the organization.

- Team meetings are the forum for deciding how to work
  together and resolve problems.

- Genuine, open relationships are encouraged so that
  employees will express their feelings, hunches, and frustrations.

- The organization fosters the emergence of participative leaders who enable the group to discuss problems and conflicts openly and constructively.

Conflict and Organization Development

Conflict propels change. Corporate raiders threaten takeovers to pressure executives to restructure organizations and raise returns to shareholders. Environmentalists challenge and embarrass corporate leaders to reduce pollution and hazards and commit resources to protect nature. Fears that competent employees will leave motivate management to involve employees more fully in decision making. Positive conflict is also vital to managing planned organizational development.

Models of Effectiveness and Intervention

Positive conflict is an ideal to which managers and employees of an effective organization must aspire. Contemporary organizations must combine their abilities and resources to continue to achieve competitive advantages. To do this, people within departments and across divisions and strategic business units must be able to use their opposing ideas to explore problems in depth and integrate apparently different ideas into elegant, effective solutions.

Positive conflict also indicates how to become an effective organization. It is through the give and take of conflict that leaders and their teams challenge outmoded ideas and approaches and find new ways of working. Once anger and frustrations are expressed, people can put that behind them and feel energized and confident that future collaboration will be productive.

The organization's culture and structure, as well as individuals' attitudes, should support positive conflict.[6] Executives and managers recognize the value of open discussions; a shared vision, a common direction, and opportunities to work as a team contribute to positive conflict. At retreats and workshops participants assess the current level of positive-conflict and brainstorm ways to strengthen the organization. Becoming a positive-conflict organization, like other great quests, requires ongoing, continuous development, and there will be barriers to overcome and conflicts to manage.

Phases of Organizational Change

There are four steps to becoming a more conflict-positive team and organization. (1)Managers and employees develop a *shared conviction* that positive conflict can be useful for them and their organizations. (2) They acquire a *common knowledge base* about managing conflict. They read about it, discuss it with one another, and as they do this together, come to see that their coworkers are becoming committed to using positive conflict. (3) They *work together* to strengthen their appreciation of their diversity, develop cooperative goals, empower each other, and take stock. They develop and implement plans to make their group more conflict-positive. (4) They encourage *continuous improvement*. Here they extend positive conflict so that people who report to them and others in the organization understand and use this technique.

Trust

Organization development's emphasis on the importance of trust and loyalty may seem out of step with the concomitant need to deal with contemporary conflicts, such as the fast-changing business realities of restructuring, plant closings, layoffs, concession-bargaining, and moving production overseas. In such critical times, long-term employment and loyalty may appear obsolete. Yet trust remains vital because today's companies need effective communication and internal commitment. With trust, people put forward their ideas and contribute to the group's work because they believe they can trust others to reciprocate. Mistrust undermines joint effort: people are wary of each other and withhold their resources and themselves. Companies that are great places to work have established strong bonds of trust.[7]

Trust is a complex idea, but fundamentally it involves feeling that one can rely on others. Trust involves disclosing information that leaves one vulnerable because others could use it exploitatively.[8] Managers demonstrate trust when they inform the union representatives about the company's financial performance and their desire for a more cooperative relationship. Union officials demonstrate trustworthiness by reciprocating with information about their major interests and by not using company information against the managers.

Conflict strengthens or destroys trust. Handling conflicts positively develops mutual reliance. Then people believe their openness has been accepted and reciprocated, have evidence that others can be trusted, and have demonstrated their own trustworthiness. The deceit of negative conflict, on the other hand, breeds mistrust.

Positive conflict gives a fresh perspective to trust. Trust need not be built on a contract that guarantees people life-time jobs and protection from change. If an organization manages conflicts openly and constructively, people will feel that they will be treated fairly and kept informed, and that their commitment will be respected and appreciated. In such an organization, security is based on the expectation that the company's managers will deal with changes openly and directly.

Positive conflict integrates "tough" and "soft" approaches to create a contemporary style of managing and organizing. Conflict-positive management is tough in that it requires confrontation of problems and struggling to work out of them. It is soft in that people must be sensitive to each other and develop strong bonds of trust. Positive conflict reconciles people and productivity. Managers and employees feel empowered when they resolve their differences and demoralized when they cannot. The company benefits by higher-quality solutions and more-facilitative procedures. Positive conflict is good for people's well-being and competence and good for a company's effectiveness.

Positive Conflict and Contemporary Leadership

Contemporary leaders are expected to take us on a journey where we want to go, but have not been before.[9] The new leadership involves courage and risk taking. This leadership is needed to create a conflict-positive organization. The outworn idea of conflict avoidance must be replaced with a realistic appreciation of the prevalence of conflict in contemporary organizations. People must see for themselves that conflict is potentially a highly constructive force, not a sinister and unwelcomed stranger.

The conflict-positive perspective clarifies the nature of contemporary leadership. It challenges the notion that strong leaders take charge by making decisions unilaterally. A strong leader establishes a climate for exploration of alternatives and honest examination of relationship frustrations. The conflict-positive view dismisses the notion of loyalty as agreement and submission. Loyal subordinates feel obligated to express their views about how their boss may be interfering with their common aspirations. Conflict-negative habits must be replaced with new ways of working together as a team.

Managers use positive conflict to be leaders. Leaders have been found to be resourceful, dedicated, and determined to succeed, yet they inspire and encourage their employees. They are flexible and spontaneous, but also pursue their vision single-mindedly. They have an entrepreneurial flair, but do not take people down a barren path. Equalitarian, they are still self-confident and assertive. Positive conflict suggests how leaders can be powerful and in charge, but also empower their employees.

Followers make a manager a leader; one cannot lead by oneself. People have to want to be inspired and led, and they want their leaders to be conflict-positive. Managers have indicated that superior leaders are honest, straightforward, broad-minded, cooperative, forward-looking and caring.[10] *Creating a positive-conflict organization is a credible way for leaders to demonstrate they are straightforward and honest, but also supportive and able to use problems to move their team forward.*

Leaders cannot lead by themselves, nor can they manage conflict alone. Leading and creating a conflict-positive organization demand joint work by managers and employees.

References

1. T. Janz and D. Tjosvold, "Costing effective vs. ineffective work relationships," *Canadian Journal of Administrative Sciences* 2 (1985): 43–51.

2. H. C. Foushee, "Dyads and triads at 35,000 feet: Factors affecting group process and aircrew performance," *American Psychologist* 39 (1984): 885–93.

3. R. R. Blake, J. S. Mouton, and A. A. McCanse, *Change by Design* (Reading, MA: Addison-Wesley, 1989).

4. D. Tjosvold, "Flight crew coordination to manage safety risks," *Group and Organization Studies* (in press).

5. M. A. Rahim, "Managing conflict in organizations." In M.A. Rahim (Ed.), *Managing Conflict: An Interdisciplinary Approach* (New York: Praeger, 1989).

6. G. A. Newman, J. E. Edwards, and W. S. Raju, "Organizational development interventions: A meta-analysis of their effects on satisfaction and other activities," *Personnel Psychology* 42 (1989): 461–89.

7. R. Levering, *A Great Place to Work* (New York: Random House, 1988).

8. M. Deutsch, *The Resolution of Conflict* (New Haven: Yale University Press, 1973).

9. J. M. Kouzes and B. Z. Posner, *The Leadership Challenge* (San Francisco: Jossey-Bass, 1987).

10. Ibid.

Part I

Confronting Conflict

Chapter 1 describes the long-standing conflict between the production and computer groups at Lee Cement. Like many other ongoing conflicts in organizations, this one had escalated from disputes over specific issues to include suspicious attitudes and assumptions. People from both groups had argued, shouted, and sworn; although outbursts of anger were now less frequent at Lee, they were not forgotten. The conflict had entered a pessimistic, sullen period. Each group felt victimized by the other; they both shared a sense of powerlessness and loss.

The conflict reflects the company's management style and environmental pressures as well as the personalities of the protagonists. Dealing with this conflict would require developing new assumptions and structuring more productive ways to collaborate.

Chapter 2 outlines the theoretical framework that can be used to break out of such ongoing conflicts. The framework also suggests how to put positive conflict to work and move an organization toward being conflict-positive.

1

Conflict's Grip

Compared with the contempt of mankind, all other external evils are easily supported.
Adam Smith

"I wish 'god' was on our side," Jake Stewart greeted Rick Hodskins, who was just arriving for the regular day shift at Lee Cement, "then we could make cement around here." Jake had migrated from Scotland to Washington State 12 years ago and had been promoted to night production supervisor four years ago. He retained a lilt in his speech and a sardonic manner.

"Don't tell me the computer had another glitch," Rick said seriously. "God" was their nickname for Michael Snyder, the head of the computer group at Lee. Rick was the production superintendent with overall responsibility for the plant. His fifty-some years still showed a powerful build, though it was now overlaid with an additional twenty pounds. His moist eyes revealed a sensitive man under pressure who might shed a tear or burst out in anger.

"I wish it were only one. How are we supposed to keep this billion dollar plant working 24 hours a day, pumping tons of materials, keeping the kiln turning at over 1,000 degrees, when the computer keeps going out? Tell me how."

"The biggest joke is that this is suppose to be a computer-driven production plant. The computer is driving us production people crazy."

"I got Dick on the phone late last night about a problem in the rolling mill, but I don't think he knew what Lee was. If he wants to drink like that on his own time it's okay, but he isn't much help to us when he's like that."

   "The guy's got to deal with 'god' every day. That can drive anyone to drink. What did you do?"

Figure 1.1
Organizational Chart at Lee

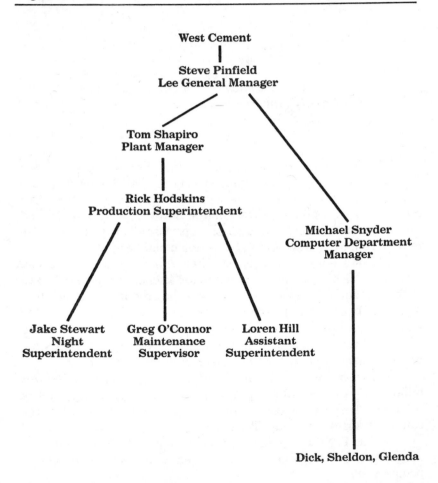

West Cement

Steve Pinfield
Lee General Manager

Tom Shapiro
Plant Manager

Rick Hodskins
Production Superintendent

Michael Snyder
Computer Department
Manager

Jake Stewart
Night
Superintendent

Greg O'Connor
Maintenance
Supervisor

Loren Hill
Assistant
Superintendent

Dick, Sheldon, Glenda

"I had to call Glenda. She had her usual 'Here-you-go-again-blaming-the-computer-because-you-don't-know-anything' voice, but I finally got some help."

"After you prove to them beyond a shadow of a doubt that there is a computer problem, they will help. They'll deal with crises."

"That's right. Don't ask them to do something to improve the system. All you get back is that the system is so much better than it was five years ago. But even I know that five years ago is ancient history when it comes to computers."

"Either that or they will say, 'No problem, have it to you in six weeks.' Six *months* later, nothing."

Jake looked out over the silos, kiln, storage areas, coal bins, conveyors, and big machines that made up the factory. He was proud to be a part of such a massive, complex undertaking as a modern cement plant. That's why he was so often frustrated. After a few moments, he said, "Can't you get those computer wizards to do something to bring us up to snuff?"

Rick shared this moment of silent commitment and pride with Jake. He just loved seeing that kiln go around; at the same time, he dreaded the thought of it stopping. Jake's question got him back to the computer people. "I'm tired of pounding the table and banging my head against the wall with them. Ask them a question, and they just tell you that you know nothing or try to blind you with science."

"It gets me so angry. Here we are, completely dependent upon the computer but knowing nothing. And the computer group isn't interested in making things better for us."

"It's like the computer is a big black box. Put something in and maybe or maybe not get something back...it may even be what you want." Behind this humor and venting, Rick wanted a way to reconcile his attitudes toward the computer group.

"Let's hardwire the place and keep the machines moving. The accountants can use the computer."

"Good idea! The computer people can find a job downtown, where they can keep banker's hours and not worry about getting dirty and mixing with people like us."

"They certainly don't care much about us or making cement."

Later that morning upstairs on the second floor of the operations building, Dick and Glenda were coming to work. From there, they had an excellent overview of the plant where Jake and Rick had been talking. Yet the view did not do justice to the scale of the plant, or the sweat it took to make it work, or the grime it created. One had to walk about it to see how massive it was and to sense how much heat and materials were consumed to make cement.

Dick had in his 54 years developed a comfortable attitude about work. He liked being in the know about computers and, while he took his job of making cement seriously, at the same time he devoted much of himself to his hobbies and pastimes. "Did you get a call from that raving Scotsman late last night?" he asked Glenda. "I couldn't even make out what the guy was talking about."

Glenda took her profession and career more seriously than Dick. At age 29 she was committed to demonstrating her competence as a computer specialist. "You should have heard him when he got to me," Glenda said. "Mostly it was a matter of pushing the right buttons, as we've told them time after time. But he also needed the new code because we had switched over to the new group start in the rolling mill. Fortunately, I was able to trouble-shoot over the phone. It's no fun coming out here in the middle of the night in the rain."

"Some of these guys have been around here so long you would think they would have learned despite themselves." Dick had no formal training in computers, but he prided himself that he had seen early in his life that electronics was moving into computers and had acquired a good working knowledge of them.

"They're not interested in learning about the computer; they just want to get through their shift and go home." Glenda was usually soft and gentle, but when she felt wronged she came out swinging.

"Doesn't it dawn on them that they will have to do another shift tomorrow?"

"They're into crises," Glenda concluded.

"Too bad they keep forgetting that the point is to make cement, not just get through the day. Isn't making cement what's it all about?"

Glenda did not want to hear Dick go on and on about making cement, and she had her own frustrations. "I think I would have called you last night if someone had to come out and troubleshoot. My kid's sick, and it seems like I've had to stay late and come out so much lately."

"Don't look at me." Dick saw himself as the one who was always called because the workers don't feel threatened by him. He at least would hang out with them in the lunch room. Glenda and the others stood back and let him take the abuse. "I get called up plenty and have to get out here in the middle of the night."

"I guess you're right," Glenda reluctantly agreed. "They call Sheldon too. But they don't call Michael. They're scared of him."

"Dealing with people is not Michael's strong suit. He knows what the computer can do for this plant, but mixing it up with the plant people is not Michael's thing."

"Let's hear no complaining about our fearless leader," Sheldon said as he entered the room. He was the most sarcastic member of the computer group. He was in rebellion with Michael and missed few opportunities to let others, including users, know his frustrations. He prided himself on being a computer professional with over ten years' experience who served users well, but was frustrated that he wasn't able to do that at Lee. He blamed Michael.

"Both Dick and I got called last night about the rolling mill's new group start," Glenda said. "Another screw up. The software wasn't complete and the supervisor down there didn't know what to do."

"Sounds vaguely familiar," Sheldon said, rolling his eyes and eyebrows up. "The names change, but the plot stays the same. And it will 'til we get some good leadership and the users get some service."

"Michael's done a lot for this plant," Dick said. "He had the vision of computer and he's carried it through."

"But he's sloppy when it comes to details," Sheldon said. "He starts some project and then tells us to finish it, which is more work and less professional than if he let us work without interference."

"It's no fun when he tells us to finish up his projects; we don't know his logic nor what the user is looking for," Glenda agreed.

"How come you don't say anything to him," Sheldon shot back to Glenda. "It's always me that he thinks is complaining."

"He's the boss...it's his department," Glenda defended.

"I don't see you going to him and talking straight much either," Dick said to Sheldon.

"We have had our share of run-ins," Sheldon said. "Besides, it wouldn't do any good—I'm the last person he wants to listen to."

There was a pause in the conversation. The three silently counted their frustrations and felt their common sense of failure. It was hard not to feel demoralized, vulnerable, and alone.

"You two really have a 'thing' going," Dick broke the silence. "Michael and I have had our problems over the years, but some time ago we hashed things out."

"He'll hash me out right out of the company...that's what he wants," Sheldon responded. "What irritates me is that everyone thinks he's Mr. Computer, and he gets whatever he wants. If he wants to go to San Diego for a seminar, he goes. If he wants new micros, he gets them. But he's just an engineer. He still does programming in Cobol. No computer professional would be caught dead doing that."

"There are frustrations," Glenda said. "You know, we don't get much praise around here. The users are always mad, and Michael isn't very positive, either."

"Welcome to Lee!" Dick exclaimed. "I can't remember a time that the plant manager or anyone from the corporate office ever personally thanked me. Sometimes you get a note on the bulletin board, but that's not the same."

"I don't need his compliments." Sheldon was defiant. "I don't like being his little appendage, his arms and legs. We're supposed to be his extensions rather than our own people. In my other jobs we were treated like professionals. Michael doesn't know how to manage professionals."

"He does like to keep a close check on us—it's his way of keeping us organized, I guess." Glenda was sympathetic to Sheldon, but she tried to understand Michael's perspective.

"We better get back to the dungeons," Sheldon said. "Michael will think we are conspiring against him if he sees us talking together and not working on his little assignments."

Tom Shapiro enjoyed the cement business and his job as plant manager at Lee. To him it was much more than a commodity business. It was high tech, low tech, and everything in between. He was outgoing, and he enjoyed the mix of people and the challenges of making cement. He felt the problems at Lee deeply, and searched for solutions tirelessly. His boss and his boss's boss, as well as the employees, were counting on him to make as much cement as possible. They could sell all they could make, though not at prices that would make corporate office content. He knew he wanted to do something about the problems between the computer group and his plant. So he walked over to Michael's office.

"Hey, Michael, do you have a few minutes?" Tom genuinely liked Michael; he did not have to pretend graciousness. They had an odd, formal relationship. Michael's group worked for Tom, but they both reported to the general manager.

"Sure, Tom, be glad to talk," Michael said. Michael reciprocated Tom's respect and ambivalence. They had been through a lot together, and Michael saw Tom as a good manager committed to making cement. This respect made Tom's public criticisms of the computer group more painful.

Michael's office reflected his interests. Computers and gadgets were jammed into his small office, giving it a cluttered look. He was into doing things through things, not getting prepared to work. He cared little for conventions, but generally went along with them, anyway. He saw no compelling reason to appear neatly organized.

"Rick was complaining again today about the computer support the production people get. I guess Jake's had a rough night, and he complained to Rick, and Rick complained to me."

"Sounds like a daytime soap opera," Michael laughed. Despite his nickname of "god," he liked to tease and laugh. Yet that label had some truth. When cornered, or when he felt he had been wronged, he could easily feel self-righteous and his humor took on a cutting edge.

"True enough, but this one we have to live with," Tom said. Tom appreciated the humor, but he wanted something done in order to somehow put the computer problems behind him.

"I'm just working on a memo that documents that the computer is getting more and more reliable. That should take some of the sting out of the complaints of production that the computer is 'The Problem.'"

"I am not sure that will get us very far." Tom's voice conveyed impatience. "They all know that we are better off, but what was good enough five years ago is not today. Expectations change." Tom felt again the old frustrations with the computer group and heard himself saying the old lines.

"But they must not understand. These guys can't remember what happened yesterday."

"I can't stop you from circulating the memo, but it's not going to help."

"I think it will be good for them to see the whole record."

"Well, I think it will be much more useful if we got some training for the production people." Realizing he was not going to persuade Michael about the computer-problems memo, Tom switched to one of his solutions for the conflict between the computer group and production. "You tell me, they tell me that they do not know that much about the computers. Surely training will help."

"I couldn't agree more. One of the big problems we have is that despite what we tell them, they keep forgetting what to do and so they call us up at all kinds of hours and we trudge out here in the middle of the night to tell them again what we have told them many times before. Dick has been out here so much."

"I know—it is not a very good situation. The production guys feel so helpless."

"The training will be good—it will show some of those guys that they don't know much about the computer and that they'd better smarten up."

"We need to take a positive approach to this, Michael." Tom said to himself, *Here he goes again, blaming my production people. Be cool because it doesn't do any good to get angry with Michael.* "Perhaps you should see if you can get a consultant to help us develop training."

"Sure thing. Thanks for stopping by."

Tom walked uneasily over to his office, and bumped into Steve Pinfield, the general manager. Steve was a throwback to the 1930s. He was a solid guy with little interest in flash. He liked making cement, and very much enjoyed being a manager and watching out for his people. He went to bat for them in dealings with the ever-changing political landscape of West Cement, the parent corporation of Lee. He acted as a buffer, a stabilizer against the overly chaotic and intrusive directives and trends of the corporate office. He had his frustrations dealing with the people in the head office, but felt it was unwise to stoke the fires of discontent by talking about them at Lee.

Steve's office and desk were large, but Tom felt quite comfortable there. He and Steve had had their battles, but for most of them, they were on the same side. He had no problem talking to Steve.

Steve knew Tom well and liked him. "You don't look happy," he said.

"Talking to Michael is not my idea of a good time. He's brilliant and he's helped the company a lot, but he can be so slippery to deal with. Perhaps he is just too brilliant for the rest of us. Maybe we need smarter managers around here." Tom tried to add some humor to his conversation.

"Michael's a smart one all right. It's too bad he shoots himself in the foot by getting people mad at him. He could go a long way in the company if he could only work with people without getting them upset."

"I've tried…you've tried to tell him that. It just doesn't sink in very far."

"I would feel a lot better if we could do something about the problem. Got any ideas?"

"I guess you're not for getting a new million dollar computer, are you?" Tom said with a laugh.

"Those guys over in the head office would love that idea. I can hear the laughter already."

"If they had their way, we would still be pushing buttons and shoveling. I know: let's tell the computer group and production people to grow up and start acting like adults."

"Now that's managing," Steve joked. "Such a delicate, sure-fire approach."

"Sure to start fires anyway." They were thankful they could laugh together.

"We should get together and talk about this soon."

"Let's." Tom wanted a solution now, but he knew that was impossible. These problems had developed over the years, and they would not disappear without a struggle. Yet, he felt good to be talking about doing something.

Reflecting on the Conflict at Lee

What occasions the greater part of the world's quarrels? Simply this: Two minds meet and do not understand each other in time enough to prevent any shock of surprise at the conduct of either party.
    John Keats

Conflict is central to working at Lee. People in production and the computer group are on guard with each other for they fear that even a small irritation will cause their frustrations to erupt to the surface. They are continually plagued by their inability to work together. The conflict makes synergy between the production and computer groups unlikely, disrupts the computer group, and challenges Michael's leadership. Their conflict interferes with making cement efficiently, with updating the technology of the plant, and with computerizing the corporation. It makes obtaining the company's targeted return on investment more uncertain.

Perspectives on the Conflict

Production employees had important grievances against the computer group. They resented the computer group's talking down to them; they were angry that the computer group did not take care of them, but left them alone to cope; they felt the computer group was not part of the team. As one veteran cement maker put it, "It's fine for Michael to have other job priorities, but he hasn't shown that he loves us first."

The computer group viewed the problem much differently. They were convinced that the production employees just wanted to get through the day and wouldn't bother to learn how to make the computer work, that they used their power as the largest group and the producer of cement to lambaste the computer group and make it feel guilty enough so that it would have to respond to their manufactured crises. All this was done to hide the production group's ignorance.

In one sense, the computer group and the production department had the same view of the conflict. There was a clear "villain" who was self-righteous, quick to blame, unresponsive to others' needs, and "unmotivated" to do much about the problem. They had just reached different conclusions about who the culprit was!

Lee's managers were caught in the conflict as well. They heard the sniping and complaints from the various players. Rick's gripes seem real and legitimate. Tom was very sympathetic to his production people and easily joined them in venting their frustrations and blaming the computer group. Yet Tom and Steve realized that not all the right was on production's side; Michael had his reasons for being irritated.

Tom and Steve felt stymied. They knew that the conflict could not be easily settled by siding with one group. In fact, they sometimes felt like lashing out at both of them, but they knew that such venting would be counterproductive. When they did let production and computer know their frustrations, the groups would get offended and begin a new round of attacks and counterattacks. Steve and Tom hoped that by nibbling away the big problem would diminish.

Losses

Conflict is often thought to involve winning and losing. Some people will get their way and win; others must necessarily lose. There are, of course, conflicts in which some people win. However, in poorly managed organizational conflicts, like the one at Lee, more often everyone loses. *Though people want to win, no one ends up winning.*

Production Group

Production was under great pressure to keep the plant working flat out because the markets would take all the cement they could make. The corporation who recently bought the plant had made it clear that it would either make a good return on its investment or find people who could. Production people liked the challenge of making as much cement as possible. They faced important obstacles, however. As a single-line plant, a problem in one part could slow up or even shut down the entire operation. The heavy equipment, materials, and intense heat could create danger in seconds.

Instead of seeing the computer as a powerful tool in their drive to be productive, they viewed it as unreliable, felt that it got in their way and caused considerable stress. Employees had to cope with a continual stream of glitches and problems. Nights of dealing with these problems with little support were very exasperating. Rick and other supervisors often had to run out in the early morning hours to try and put things back together again. They always felt on call; some complained that they did not sleep deeply at night or relax on weekends because they might have to deal with a crisis. This pressure took a toll on their health and emotional well-being. They had less time and energy to think about how to make the plant more productive and improve the quality of work for their employees.

They felt trapped. They knew they were vulnerable because they were so heavily dependent upon the computer, yet their knowledge and skills were inadequate. Nor did they feel they could rely on the computer group. They felt guilty for avoiding the computer group and letting issues slide. They knew they were contributing to the unreliability of the computer system and their own problems with productivity.

The conflict got in the way of their learning and becoming more proficient with the computer. There were few discussions about what the production people wanted, what they needed to know to make the system work, and how they could use the computer to help them. Production and computer people avoided talking, and when they did talk it was usually regarding a specific problem that needed to be dealt with immediately. Suggestions from the computer people on what production could do next time were thought to be put-downs or more evidence that the computer group did not want to work with them and were avoiding their responsibility to serve users.

Computer Group

The computer group suffered too. They also operated in a crisis mode, ready to troubleshoot anytime day or night. They felt unappreciated. Their goal was to make the computer valuable, but their primary "customers" were unhappy and hostile. They felt overwhelmed and surrounded by a much more powerful, antagonistic group. They knew they could do much more for the company, but complaints from production held them back. Michael's responsibilities were curtailed, and the computer group had few opportunities to demonstrate their worth, carry on with computerization of the corporation, and gain stature and promotions.

The conflict splintered the computer group. While they wanted to defend their group, it was tempting at times to agree with the users and blame Michael or others in the group. They were divided and dispirited.

Lee Cement

Lee and Tom and Steve lost in many ways. The corporation wanted a good return on its large investment in the plant facilities. Tom and Steve knew that in addition to high production levels they had to maintain quality. If the company got a reputation that its cement was difficult to work with, customers would go elsewhere. Cement that could not be formed properly or would dry too quickly or too slowly was worth little.

Shortcomings with the computer threatened both the production and the quality of the cement. The production lost through a computer glitch could not be made up—that time was gone. Cement that was not mixed properly or fired at the right temperature had to be recycled, some of it dumped. Some low-quality cement made its way to the marketplace.

The conflict threatened the future productivity of the plant. Some supervisors had health problems and ulcers that would eventually undermine their performance. Experienced workers began to think of leaving the company. The loss of skilled, experienced employees could be devastating to the highly automated plant.

The conflict was interfering with the computerization and updating of the company and the corporation. Other managers were unsympathetic to new ways to use the computer. They wanted the process system to work better before the computer group could do more for the accountants and office staff. Nor were Tom and Steve open to the computer group helping other plants in the corporation computerize. The conflict distracted people from looking to the future and thinking about how to make the plant work better. The company had experienced a seven-month strike five years ago in which the plant stood idle. Recent negotiations had gone better, but there were feelings of resentment and "us against them." The managers and supervisors had not devoted the energy to turning these attitudes around. Labor relations were a time bomb that might begin ticking at any time.

Lee had the additional vulnerability of being highly dependent upon Michael's computer knowledge. People outside the computer group were not well versed in the computer, and even those inside the group had narrow areas of competence. Steve and Tom worried about what they would do if they lost Michael's services voluntarily or involuntarily. They knew that the continued hostility toward Michael could lead to his wanting to find a different job. Michael resented complaints about the computer as ungrateful carping that failed to appreciate his years of work for the company. He was thinking of leaving, but did not want to leave the company devoid of computer knowledge.

The conflict between production and the computer group increased Lee's uncertainties and vulnerabilities. These costs were not marginal, or "soft." Indeed, many of them could be measured in "bottom-line" terms. Employees, supervisors, and managers spent a great deal of their paid time coping with computer related problems. The conflict led to reduced production and revenues. The costs of turnover in terms of training new people and loss of production were real. The company's inattention to its labor climate could cost it dearly in the future.

Production employees and the computer group knew very well that the conflict was costly. It was easy for them to feel that they were the big loser and to be much less sensitive to the other group's losses. They assumed that if the other group was not benefiting in some way, it would have done something about the conflict.

The Deadlock

The conflict at Lee had persisted for years. Managers as well as researchers often conclude that the reason problems are not solved is because people are not motivated, that they really don't care enough. However, the people at Lee, as in many important conflicts, did care and were looking for solutions.

Indeed, they were too solution-minded. Rick thought the computer group should be at the plant 24 hours a day; Jake dreamed of hardwiring the plant. Michael wanted the production people to be more aware of the history of the computer at Lee and to appreciate the progress that had been made. Tom thought training the production workers was an answer.

There were many solutions proposed, but few were implemented. One side dismissed the other's proposals. Even accepted solutions were implemented half-heartedly. The failure of these attempts to improve the situation, combined with their ongoing frustrations, fed a deep sense of powerlessness that they could not solve the problem.

Their sense of powerlessness was in part highly realistic. Production, the computer group, and even the managers attempted to solve the conflict from their own standpoint and by their own efforts. However, these independent attempts were doomed because conflicts need to be solved together. Solutions proposed by one side would likely be biased and even more likely to be considered biased. *They could not work together to untangle their conflict.*

The poorly managed conflict at Lee frustrated Steve and Tom's efforts to make the plant more productive and the people more motivated, Michael's career as a manager of technology, the computer group's opportunities for new challenges and promotions, and the production group's drive to make cement and improve the labor climate. Unmanaged conflict is such a destructive force because it undermines the ability of people to communicate and solve problems, including how they manage their conflicts. Yet the people at Lee, as described in the following chapters, began to work together to take charge of their conflict.

What Is Conflict?

Conflict is part of leading, following, doing, and thinking in an organization. Conflict is inevitable in organizations as people with different responsibilities, training, and outlook try to coordinate. Conflict is so pervasive that it has been difficult to define. There is a great deal of conflict among social scientists about how conflict can best be defined.

Conflict is defined here as incompatible activities and behaviors.[1] One person's behavior is thought to be obstructing and interfering with another's. Rick's demand that a person from the computer group be at the plant 24 hours a day is incompatible with Michael's plans to protect his group and his own family time, and therefore they are in conflict. There is conflict when Sheldon argues that Dick should buy more expensive computer parts and Dick resists in order to protect his budget.

Conflict is often thought to be bargaining and negotiation where protagonists have opposing interests and goals. What one wants opposes and frustrates what others want. Although they have a common interest in reaching an agreement, they have competitive interests regarding what proposal should be adopted.

While many conflicts call for negotiation and bargaining, not all conflict is based on opposing goals. People with common, cooperative goals often have a great deal of conflict. Rick and Michael share the same goal of having a reliable computer system and will both benefit when the system works without crashes and crises. Yet they are in continual disagreement about how they should achieve that goal. They fight about who is to blame, who should pay, and who should take the first steps to initiate joint problem solving. Overlapping, cooperative goals do not minimize conflict.

Nor is there a direct link between opposing interests and conflict. *Conflicts do not just appear; people construct them.* People have to decide whether someone is interfering with them. The computer group may all want a first-class design for a new program. Dick may find Sheldon's humor a useful release of tension and laugh; Glenda may be upset because she sees the humor as interfering with brainstorming and getting the job done. Opposing goals have little to do with their conflict. Expectations, perceptions, and evaluations all affect whether people experience conflict.

People make choices about conflict. They decide whether, and to what extent, they are in conflict. For example, if Glenda concludes that Sheldon is intentionally trying to delay their work, perhaps because he wants to show Michael that it would be better to give him the assignment, she might become agitated and suspicious. However, if she assumes that Sheldon's just expressing his good-natured self, she may decide to tease back and ask him to get back on track.

Conflict is not synonymous with violence, arguments, and anger. It may be expressed in these ways, but it is also expressed in laughing, teasing, silence, and affection. Conflict does not itself compel one kind of behavior. Employees may hide their feelings, suppress their thoughts, and bite their tongues, but they will still be in conflict. However, they need not feel trapped. They have choices and options in how they experience conflict and how they express themselves and manage their conflicts. Conflict presents opportunities and challenges.

Conflict Is Built in to Organizations

Conflict is often attributed to the styles and aggressiveness of individuals. Managers who criticize publicly pain sensitive employees. Quiet, sullen employees upset a boss who wants to feel appreciated. There are self-centered, "nasty" people who seem to enjoy pricking and annoying others. Some highly aggressive people do not care who they climb over to get to the top. There is a growing appreciation that the variety of personal styles in an organization must be accommodated. Less appreciated is the fact that *conflict is part of the very purpose and rationale of organizations.*

Organizations touch every aspect of life; we work, worship, relax, exercise, and eat in them. An organization is a network of relationships designed to accomplish established goals. It takes people and resources from the environment, uses them to create products, and markets these products to the environment. An organization thus requires:

1. Skilled employees motivated to transform the resources into products.

2. The ability to identify obstacles, solve problems, and take advantage of opportunities.

3. Strategies to market products and adapt to the environment.

4. A management process that integrates the people and resources into an effective system to achieve organizational goals.[2]

Conflict is part of achieving these requirements. Employees who lack skills or motivation need to be challenged to develop them. Organizational members are going to have different and opposing views about obstacles, problems, opportunities, and how the organization should respond. They will disagree about the best ways to market products, the nature of needed changes, and how these changes should be implemented. Managers spend a good part of each day trying to anticipate and deal with these conflicts.[3]

Organizations combine the talents and motivations of many to accomplish goals individuals cannot achieve acting alone. No one person has the knowledge and energy to make cement, design and build a new airplane, or explore space. Investing, making cookies, and building cars benefit from organized effort—indeed, there are few tasks that don't.

The power of organized effort is based on the division of labor and specialization. All organizations divide work, but they use many different principles. Some companies divide work by product lines and assign a group the responsibility for each line. Others assign major tasks to the departments of production, marketing, research, and administration. A contemporary approach is matrix organization, where people belong to functional groups such as engineering and marketing, but also work on project teams.

With independent responsibilities, departments and individuals concentrate on their work and can develop the expertise to contribute successfully to the company. This specialization works for individuals because they can feel a sense of mastery as they do their jobs well. Today's organizations are increasingly dependent upon computer, financial, marketing, production, and other specialists. Companies also cross national boundaries, and ask people with different ethnic and political backgrounds to work together.

Inevitably people with different responsibilities, training, and positions are going to reach different, and at times opposing, views. The very diversity of backgrounds and perspectives that the organization requires and encourages results in conflict. *The irony is that most organizations want their employees to pretend that they are not in conflict; the agony of employees is that they cannot.*

Concluding Comments

Production and computer groups at Lee had been fighting each other for years. Production felt the computer group was getting in their way of making cement; the computer people felt that production was sabotaging their efforts to update the plant's technology. This conflict heightened the divisions within the computer group.

Attempts to resolve the conflict were one-sided. Each wanted the other to recognize their errors and change. They avoided, blamed, and argued. They saw their conflict as a confrontation to be avoided or a battle to be won.

The people at Lee wanted to improve their systems. Steve and Tom believed that improving the climate would increase the quality and production of cement. Michael wanted a worry-free computer system, and production aimed for maximum output. The computer employees wanted greater autonomy and more input in decisions. Positive conflict can further these aspirations by using opposition to generate solutions. The next chapter introduces the Conflict-Positive Model.

References

1. M. Deutsch, *The Resolution of Conflict* (New Haven, CT: Yale University Press, 1973).

2. D. Tjosvold and D.W. Johnson (Eds.), *Productive Conflict Management: Implications for Organizations* (Minneapolis: Team Media, 1989).

3. K.W. Thomas and W.H. Schmidt, "A survey of managerial interests with respect to conflict," *Academy of Management Journal,* 19(1976): 315–18.

2

Positive Conflict: Theory and Research

Conflict is the gadfly of thought. It stirs us to observation and memory. It instigates invention. It shocks us out of sheeplike passivity, and sets us at noting and contriving ....[C]onflict is a "sine qua non" of reflection and ingenuity.

> John Dewey, *Human Nature and Conduct: Morals are Human*

Tom wanted a solution to the computer problems. The ongoing bickering was a legacy and an unwelcome reminder of a turbulent past. He and Steve had been through some rough times, especially during the seven-month strike five years ago that left the plant idle and ruined lives. They had committed themselves to building an effective organization that avoided such disruptions.

Yet he doubted that there was an easy solution, or even one solution to the squabbling between the groups at Lee. One of Tom's MBA professors suggested that Dale Nordlund, a colleague who studied organizational conflict, may be able to help. Dale had sent Tom articles arguing that conflict was inevitable in organizations, and that good managers and companies learned how to make conflict useful and positive.

Tom found the idea of managing conflict appealing. Like most managers, he had assumed that conflict and managing were opposites, and he found it intellectually stimulating to try to understand how they could go together. He thought managing conflict might be practical as well.

Tom had discussed with Steve the idea of bringing in a consultant on conflict and gave Steve the articles to look over. Steve liked the idea of managing conflict too. In his decades in the mining and cement business, Steve had worked with many production people who like Rick and Jake were quick to express their anger. His recent years in general management had given him more experience with accountants, computer programers, and other professionals. They got angry too.

Steve asked Tom to run the idea of a conflict consultant past Michael. Steve wanted to avoid the appearance that, under Tom's insistence, he was forcing something on Michael. He wanted Michael to be receptive and to devote the time and energy needed to make this human-relations-management program work. Michael was interested, and Tom had lunch with Dale and had him talk with Michael.

"You remember that the conflict researcher is supposed to be here in a few minutes?" Tom asked as he walked into Steve's office.

"I'm looking forward to it," Steve said. "I think we're better at dealing with conflicts than we were. I guess we couldn't get much worse than a seven-month strike—it still pains me to think about that."

"How could we have gotten into such a quagmire?" Tom asked, without wanting or expecting an answer.

Steve rocked his head back and forth and looked out his window for a second, and then got back to the issue at hand. "Well, let's hope a program in managing conflict can get the computer and production people working with, not against, each other. We could certainly use better conflict in other areas of the company too."

"Managing conflict addresses at least part of the problem," Tom said. "What I found interesting was the idea that managers cannot expect to set up a structure where everything works perfectly, but that we should help them so that they discuss issues and conflicts that come along. That's realistic."

"This professor we're meeting with today . . . Dale Nordlund . . . the one you had lunch with the other day . . . has he actually been studying conflict?" Steve asked.

"I'm surprised too, but he says there has been quite a lot of research on conflict in the last thirty years and it's beginning to pay off," Tom said.

"I like the idea, but changing the way we deal with conflict won't be easy," Steve said.

"You know how I feel," Tom said. "We need someone who really understands the idea. Otherwise we might botch it up and blame the idea when it was really that we didn't know how to use it properly."

"Perhaps we should know everything about managing and about conflict, but we don't," Steve said matter of factly. "We might be part of the problem."

"That thought had crossed my mind. We've both given him advice to try to solve the problem, but we may be part of it."

Steve's secretary announced that Dale Nordlund had arrived and showed him in. After greeting each other, Tom said laughingly, "Did you see any conflicts as you came in the door?"

"I don't think we have people biting each other, at least not yet," Steve joined in. "I did notice two people smoking outside," Dale deadpanned. "Did you send them out for misbehaving?" Dale had discovered his niche in studying and talking about conflict. He found conflict intellectually challenging and practically useful, but also lively and fun. Conflict opens up situations and people. It gets to the heart of what's going on in an organization. Talking about conflict is a way for people to reveal their values and personalities. Dale liked the give and take, the honesty and humor of dealing with conflict.

"That's our new nonsmoking policy at work," Steve explained. "We had a vote to ban it...I suppose some day we should find a space for them to smoke inside. It can get cold in the winter. We ex-smokers are tough."

"There's conflict everywhere," Dale said. "Smoking... whatever."

"*That* there is," Tom said, nodding his head. "You've had a chance to talk to Michael, and I've gone over your proposal with Steve, but why don't you give us an overview, Dale."

"I had a good talk with Michael, but before we talk about the details of the plan, I would like to discuss my basic approach," Dale began. "That will help you understand me better and what I'll be trying to do. Also, it is useful for us to talk about the nature of our contract and relationship. I hope that's okay."

"If you ask a professor over, you should be prepared for a lecture," Tom deadpanned and then broke into a quick, full smile.

"I'll keep it short, but there will be a quiz at the end," Dale said. More laughter.

Dale explained that his position is that conflict's been given a bum rap. It is not only inevitable and built into organizations, but it is also extremely useful. Indeed, if everyone thought the same way, then most organizations could use many fewer people. But organizations need specialists in marketing, production, research, and computers. The key to management is to bring them all together.

"Many people get confused about ends and means. They think that a company should be united, should be one," Dale continued. "People should share values and vision, and work together to get things done. So far so good, but then they go the next step and say that people should be harmonious all the time. My point is that you cannot expect to be at one until people have had a chance to share their differences and frustrations. Harmony needs to be worked out, not imposed.

"This confusion of ends and means shows up in decision making," Dale continued. "We want everyone on board and committed to a decision, but again that consensus needs to be hammered out by people discussing opposing views. As a Chinese proverb goes, 'Begin with certainties, end with uncertainties, Begin with uncertainties, end with certainties.' "

"I like the point you make in one of those articles about how much time and energy goes into trying to avoid conflict," Steve said. "I can see that a lot. Actually it's taken me a long time to realize that avoiding conflict does not work. Just ask my wife!"

"People really do work at avoiding conflict," Tom said. "But what are they supposed to do instead?"

"In a word, manage," Dale said.

"Easier said than done," Tom said.

"It can get very complicated, but in a way, managing conflict is very basic—we all have to deal with conflict, and you wouldn't be where you are today if you weren't pretty good at it, at least some of the time for some conflicts."

"I think he's saying we're not behind bars," Steve said.

"Dealing with some people is more difficult than others—which gets us back to Michael," Tom said with a laugh.

Dale handed out diagrams of positive, win-lose, and avoid approaches to conflict, and explained that it is useful to examine conflict between individuals and departments, and that it also has implications for making decisions and leading an organization. It has four related parts: valuing diversity, sharing aspirations, empowering, and taking stock.

Dale argued that people in organizations should *recognize, even celebrate, their diversity.* They should realize that no one person has the right answer, but that contemporary organizations need many different kinds of specialists. Deciding what an organization should do requires these diverse views.

But people should not confuse differences with opposing interests. Just because marketing sees a problem differently than production does not mean that they are fighting against each other and that their goals are incompatible. In fact, the key to managing

Figure 2.1
Positive Conflict

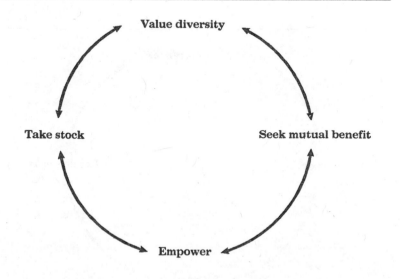

Figure 2.2
Competitive Conflict

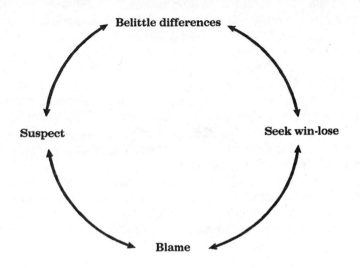

Figure 2.3
Avoid Conflict

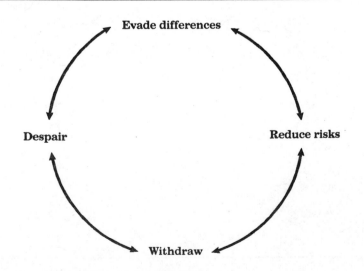

conflict is to discuss differences openly with the understanding that people have *overlapping goals and are seeking "win-win" solutions.* Marketing and production both want a prosperous company that gives them pride and security, but they have very different ideas about how to get there. Shared visions, group tasks, win-win rewards, and believing they are on the same side all help give employees cooperative goals and help manage their conflicts.

Empowering is the third step. Employees need forums and settings in which they have the time and encouragement to express their frustrations and various ideas. Task forces, quality circles, department meetings, performance appraisals, open-door policies, and managing by walking around can provide opportunities. Managing conflict is challenging, and people need skills and the confidence to use them. Often in poorly managed conflict, people have had few opportunities to deal with conflict openly and have come to feel powerless and unable.

Periodically, groups and organizations should *take stock and reflect on how they are managing conflict.* They can check to see if they are valuing their differences and speaking out, if they are maintaining a strong sense of cooperative goals, if they have opportunities, and if they are strengthening their skills. Developing a positive-conflict organization is not a simple one- or two-step procedure. People have to work at conflict and strive for continuous improvement to value diversity, share aspirations, and empower.

Most situations can easily slip into *competitive, win-lose conflict.* In such conflicts, people accuse others of being difficult, obstructive, and irrational. They focus on getting their own individual task completed and think in terms of competitive, win-lose goals; their shared vision and common mission seem vague and distant. They believe the only way they can influence the other is through coercion and manipulation. They may be highly frustrated, blame others, and righteously seek to undermine, even sabotage, their antagonists. On occasions when they do feel they are winning, they worry that the "losers" will turn on them.

The third alternative is to *avoid conflict.* In their effort to evade frustrations and difficulties, people forgo their aspirations for the relief of reducing risks. They smooth over differences and psychologically withdraw. These short-term strategies can produce a sense of despair and a feeling that they are powerless to deal with problems.

Though they generate contrasting behaviors, *"competitive" and "avoid" are two sides and forms of negative conflict.* Many people, including the production and computer groups at Lee, alternate between them. The antagonists may first blame and demand, and as these strategies fail, they then try to avoid and smooth over the difficulties. However, as ignoring seldom solves underlying problems and frustrations, they later vent their anger and demand change.

"In a way, making conflict positive is simple, but on the other hand, you're really talking about a whole way of thinking about organizations and managing," Tom said.

"It is not a simple one- or two-step program, or a few techniques," Dale said.

"Too bad," Steve concluded. "I like simple solutions. I'm wondering how practical this is. We have people who've been fighting for years and don't trust each other. If one says it's white, the other says it's black."

"Managing conflict is practical," Dale said. "It does not require that people love and respect and trust each other. If they don't, then we can focus on the issue of mistrust. Most tough conflict has to do with these kinds of attitude and relationship issues.

"What appears to be happening at Lee is not just conflict over computer glitches, but each side is angry with how the other communicates and deals with conflict. The production people think the computer group is arrogant; the computer group thinks the production people are throwing their weight around. They are each complaining about how the other deals with conflict. So we will need to deal with these attitudes as well as with the computer glitches."

"Let me see if I got that," Steve said. "You're saying that both groups are angry over how the other deals with them and their conflicts."

"Right. The whole process of communicating and managing conflict has broken down, and so the conflict just grinds away."

"I'm wondering, though, if we can really get them to have a shared aspiration," Tom said. "If they did, we probably won't need you here."

"Cooperative goals tend to get lost when conflicts escalate," Dale said. "In addition to the obvious common goals like making cement, each group has a very concrete common goal of ending the unproductive conflict. They both are paying a big price, I suspect. We want both groups to work together and begin to communicate to solve their common problem, namely, the ineffective conflict between them."

"You have to remember that not all of these people are college graduates," Steve said. "I don't think a super-rational approach will work."

Dale explained that managing conflict is both rational and emotional. Conflicts have rough edges; dealing with them is not a smooth, tidy process. But managing conflict is basic, and it does not require formal education. "In fact, I sometimes find that people with fewer degrees deal with conflicts more directly, emotionally, and effectively."

"I can see that," Steve said. "Corporate head offices can be the place where conflicts are handled the worst. High-priced people can spend a lot of their time posturing and in-fighting."

"I've seen corporate offices where people say they are being tough businesspeople, but they are really just gossiping and avoiding conflict," Dale said. "They find elaborate ways of fighting each other, while pretending not to, rather than dealing directly with each other."

"That sort of thing wouldn't happen at West Cement, though," Tom winked at Steve.

"Oh, no, not here." Steve let out a visible sigh. "Let's say that some people who need a managing conflict program don't see that they need one."

"I take it this model has some research behind it," Tom said. "How widely does it apply?"

"We could have more research, but we have quite a bit of support," Dale said. "The model is powerful in that it applies to many kinds of conflicts and relationships. *The model shows where we want to go*—the kind of work relationships we want between the computer group and production group as well as within these groups. *The model also shows how we are going to get there.* We want the groups to understand and accept each other's perspective on the conflict and how they should work together. We want them to see that they have common goals of ending the ineffective conflict, managing their conflicts more productively, making cement, and making Lee a productive, secure place to work. We also will be setting up brainstorming sessions, planning, and informal visits for them and sharpening their skills in managing conflict. They can also meet periodically to discuss their relationship and how it can be improved."

"Let's make sure I understand this," Tom said. "You're saying that positive conflict is both the end and the means. It's where we want to go and how we're going to get there."

"Yes, that's right," Dale said. "We can measure our success by the extent to which people at Lee are making their conflicts positive. I expect that will improve productivity, but the most direct measure of the program is the extent to which people are managing their conflicts.

"One more thing: *The model shows how I can work with you and others in the organization.* We will have conflict. We will at times have opposing and different views; sometimes I will do things that puzzle, frustrate, even irritate you and others. That's inevitable. But we have a common, shared goal to make Lee a more productive and humane place to work. I'm working for the two of you, but also for Michael, the production people, everyone here. We are working together for a mutual goal. Periodically we should sit down and discuss how we're doing and how we can work together better."

"So if we have our differences, I should let you know straight out, and not just stop sending your checks," Steve said smiling.

"Let's keep in touch and discuss our views and if you don't think we have positive conflict, then we should sit down and talk about it," Dale said. "If I don't think so, I'll let you know."

"You've given us a great deal to think about," Steve said.

Conflict-Positive Model

Existence as struggle, life as a battle, everything in terms of defeat and victory: Man versus Nature, Man versus Woman, Black versus White, Good versus Evil, God versus Devil—a sort of apartheid view of existence, and of literature. What a pitiful impoverishment of the complexity of both!
    Ursula K. Le Guin

There are four critical, interrelated aspects to managing conflict in organizations:

1. Value diversity and confront differences.
2. Seek mutual benefits and unite behind cooperative goals.
3. Empower employees to feel confident and skillful.
4. Take stock to reward success and learn from mistakes.

Value Diversity

There is no more certain sign of a narrow mind, of stupidity, and of arrogance, than to stand aloof from those who think differently from us.
Walter Savage Landor
To do nothing at all is the most difficult thing to do in the world...
Oscar Wilde

Michael, Rick, and others at Lee Cement will find it much easier to deal with diverse viewpoints and perspectives when they believe that it is a natural, normal part of working. They can recognize that diverse experiences and efforts help them understand issues more deeply and create innovative solutions to exploit opportunities and adapt to new realities.

Often employees are frustrated and upset just because others are different and look at problems from their own point of view. They worry that something is amiss, and that differences will get in their way. People often think they should work with others who will "fit in" and think alike. This harmony is counterproductive as it shortchanges the group of needed resources and perspectives. It is also unrealistic. People working together on a common problem will disagree about how much they should study the issue, whom to ask for assistance, how much change is needed, and so on. *The goal is not how to avoid differences but how to use them to accomplish common aspirations as effectively as possible.*

Confrontation. Open confrontation to bring out diverse views about issues is critical for positive conflict. Through dialogue, employees clarify the confusions and assumptions that make them suspicious. People who confront the issues develop an understanding of each other's perspective, gather information, and identify opportunities and threats. Then they are prepared to work to take advantage of opportunities and cope with threats.

Confrontation must be done skillfully and appropriately so that both sides dig into issues and problems. Surprises, insults, and confusions need to be avoided. Open discussion does not mean letting everything hang out, nor is it an excuse for dumping on others.

Confrontation demands open-mindedness. Both sides should be open to others as well as open with their own ideas and feelings. They should listen to understand others' grievances and frustrations and put themselves in the others' shoes. They should question the validity of their own ideas and appreciate that others' points of view are legitimate and important.

Seek Mutual Benefit

Once you hear the details of a victory, it is hard to distinguish it from a defeat.
Jean-Paul Sartre

Together we stand, divided we fall!
Watchword of the American Revolution

You can go out and preach common goals and work at it. . . .But you can bring your credibility down in a second. It takes a million acts to build it up, but one act can bring it down. . . .People are suspicious because for several thousand years that suspicion was warranted. So it's fragile. And we try very hard to try not to do things that will create distrust.
Howard K. Sperlich, President, Chrysler Corporation

People often try to take charge and solve a conflict by themselves. However, they may not really know what the problem is: they may work to give another a service, when the other really wants to feel appreciated. Sometimes people exacerbate conflict when they try to solve it themselves: they make additional arguments that alienate others further. *Conflicts need to be managed together.*

To the extent that employees believe that they have cooperative goals, they are able to manage their conflicts. Although they disagree, interfere, and frustrate each other and at times may think they are working at cross-purposes, they realize and frame the issues so that they believe their goals are much more compatible than opposing. They focus on concrete, common goals that provide important benefits for all. They are committed to the company's vision and want to serve its customers well. They want to resolve the conflict for mutual benefit.

Cooperative goals and conflict are highly compatible. Through conflict, people become more aware of how they depend on each other and learn that by working together they can all be better off. They find out what binds them together and discover ways that they can promote each other's goals.

Employees who agree on where they want to go will disagree about how to get there. They will have opposing views regarding the best route to take, miscommunicate and miscoordinate, and disagree about how to share the benefits and burdens. Yet if they feel they are all trying to move down the same path, they will work out these differences, indeed, use them to be more successful.

Assigning groups of diverse people to important, high-profile tasks reinforces talk of diversity and shared aspirations. Accountants, staff, and managers can devise new reporting procedures. They are charged with the common, cooperative task of developing procedures that work for everyone and that promote company objectives. They are asked to dig into the issues and develop alternatives and to use their opposing perspectives and ideas to do so.

Joint rewards back up talk of the value of diversity and assigning common tasks to diverse people. Executives publicly praise the task force as a whole and celebrate if it develops effective reporting procedures. The new-product team of engineers, marketing, production, and sales are given bonuses to the extent that their product is successful in the marketplace. People are rewarded cooperatively and together (though not necessarily equally). They share the responsibility for failures and mistakes rather than find a scapegoat to blame.

Empower

I never got very far until I stopped imagining I had to do everything myself.
    Frank W. Woolworth

Giving is the secret of a healthy life. Not necessarily money, but whatever a man has of encouragement and sympathy and understanding.
    John D. Rockefeller, Jr.

*Mutual respect is what sustains extraordinary group efforts. Leaders create an atmosphere of trust and human dignity. They nurture self-esteem in others. They make others feel strong and capable.**
    James Kouzes and Barry Posner, *The Leadership Challenge*

---

* Reprinted with permission from James Kouzes and Barry Posner, *The Leadership Challenge* (San Francisco: Jossey-Boss, 1987).

Managing conflict is something that people do for themselves; it is not done to or at them. They must feel confident that they can deal with their differences productively. They are in charge of their conflicts; their conflicts do not control them.

Making conflict positive is difficult. People are asked to communicate their ideas and feelings openly and honestly, and to be open to others. *Managing conflict has rough edges.* It is seldom a smooth process and seldom takes place without ruffled feelings and raised voices. People are going to feel angry, ignored, and unappreciated. At times, they have to deal with hostile, self-righteous fighters. Managers and employees need ongoing training in communication, negotiation, creativity, and other conflict skills.

People have been asked and rewarded much more for ignoring their differences and avoiding conflicts than for using them to get things done. They will need successful experiences and assistance to refine these skills and feel empowered.

Employees need settings and situations in which they can deal directly and openly with their conflicts. Scheduled sessions, informal meetings in the coffee room and offices, and weekend retreats are used to deal with frustrations and develop strong relationships. People feel free to call each other up and stop by the office to discuss issues and deal with conflicts before they are allowed to grow and simmer. Task forces and other teams provide a forum for people with diverse backgrounds, opinions, and viewpoints to work on common projects and integrate their perspectives to get things done.

Integration. Positive conflict requires that all perspectives be considered. *The issue is not who is right or who is wrong, or who wins and who loses, but how can the best ideas be combined to further the most pressing needs.* The solution adopted is often something quite different than originally proposed but comes out of the mix, stimulation, and reflection that occurs in well-managed conflict.

Emotions and people should also be integrated. Conflict often makes people feel separated and apart; they are angry and they focus on their differences and grievances. After the conflict, they should feel more closely connected and linked. They feel more supported and valued by each other; they have met the test of conflict. They are confident that in the future they will work together productively and warmly.

Take Stock

For things we have to learn by doing them, we learn by doing them.
   Aristotle

Habits can't be thrown out the upstairs window. They have to be coaxed down the stairs one step at a time.
   Mark Twain

People reflect on their work and relationships to identify their progress and weaknesses. They get feedback on their progress and success and on how they are working together and managing their conflicts. They talk directly about their communication and relationships so that they can strengthen their team and its members.[1]

Employees show they appreciate each other, identify each other's strengths, and build upon them. They also recognize problems and wage conflicts to resolve them. They reward and celebrate their successes and make realistic plans for how they can improve. In this way, they become self-regulating and can work on future tasks without a great deal of intervention by their superiors.

Valuing diversity, sharing aspirations, empowering, and taking stock are mutually reinforcing. Employees can begin at any phase but need to include all phases. Cooperative tasks and relationships are important, for example, but not sufficient for positive conflict. As they go through these phases, people become increasingly confident and skillful and require less assistance to use their conflicts positively.

Research Support

Research studies have formed a solid base of knowledge about conflict and its management. Morton Deutsch first laid out his theory of cooperation and competition in the 1940s, and since then many social scientists have empirically supported and developed it. The approach has proved an elegant, powerful way to understand conflict. Deutsch argued that working with others can be distinguished by how people believe they depend upon each other. How goals are related consistently and dramatically affects interaction, in particular managing conflict.[2]

People in conflict can conclude that their goals are cooperative or competitive. In cooperation, people believe that their goals are compatible and positively related; as one moves toward attaining a goal that helps others reach their goals. They may have a common goal: task force members will all be successful when Steve seriously considers their recommendations. Or they may have different goals: Rick pleases the accounting department by using its procedures so that he can develop budgets the corporate office takes seriously.

People who believe they have cooperative goals are likely to manage their conflicts productively. They recognize that it is in everyone's self-interest to promote each other's effectiveness. Feeling trusting, they freely speak their minds, reveal their frustrations, and talk about their anger. The participants welcome these confrontations and realize it is important to work out settlements so that they can continue to assist each other. They work for mutually beneficial solutions that maintain and strengthen the relationship. They explore each other's perspectives, creatively integrate their views, and are confident they will continue to work together for mutual benefit. As a result, they are prepared to collaborate and discuss future conflicts.

Competitive goals, on the other hand, make managing conflict very difficult and often lead to escalating, debilitating fights.[3] People have competitive goals when they see that their aspirations and objectives are incompatible and negatively related; the progress of one interferes with or prevents others from being successful. If task-force members see their goals as proving that they have better ideas than each other and their ideas must dominate, they are in competition. If the accountants believe they must force Rick to use the budgeting process because he wants to avoid being responsible, they are in competition.

People with competitive goals suspect that self-interest will lead to mutual frustration. They doubt that others are interested in their feelings and frustrations and fear ridicule. Although they often prefer to avoid conflict, especially with their bosses and others with authority and power, the underlying problems continue to frustrate them. If they do decide on confrontation, they often behave in a tough, dominating manner that escalates the conflict. Whether they choose to avoid or confront conflict, they usually feel that they have lost and only hope that others have lost more.

Compatible goals support valuing differences and confronting them openly and also support the skills to listen and integrate these views. At the same time, dealing with conflicts constructively demonstrates and convinces the people involved that they have cooperative goals. Dale was working to get Lee people into this cycle of positive conflict.

Conflict and Running a Company

Conflict is essential to managing an organization. The dynamics and effects of positive conflict contribute to the requirements for an effective organization. Recent studies document specifically that well-managed conflict gets ordinary and extraordinary things done for organizations.

Innovation

The demands of the marketplace and workplace require organizations to innovate and adapt. They are experimenting with new procedures and management styles, and are developing new products and services to respond to technological advances, competition, and consumer preferences. Conflict management is essential for successful innovation.

Faculty members and employees of a large post–secondary educational institution were interviewed on when they were able to solve problems in new and creative ways, and when they were frustrated in trying to develop a new approach.[4] When they discussed their opposing views openly and forthrightly and considered all views, they were able to develop innovative solutions. When they discussed issues from only one point of view and were unable to incorporate different views, then they failed to make progress and developed solutions low on quality and creativity.

Managers have long complained that employees resist new technological innovations and that, as a consequence, the investments do not pay off in the expected productivity increases. Less recognized is that employees must identify problems and discuss solutions in order to use the technology. Employees of a retail chain were found to be able to use new scanning technology more efficiently when they exchanged information and hammered out ideas about how to solve the many problems that the technology created.[5]

Managers are restructuring and transforming organizations. They are cutting management levels, splitting up businesses, forming links across business units, and using task teams and parallel structures to create synergy. However, restructuring seldom results in the expected improved quality of products, productivity, and quality of work life for employees and returns for shareholders. A large telecommunications high-technology firm had undergone waves of restructuring without noticeable improvement. Interviews revealed that changing structures was insufficient.[6] Employees had to make use of any new order, and to do this, they had to coordinate and manage their conflicts. When they were able to manage their difficulties and reassure and support each other, they were able to make use of new structures.

Guides for Action

Value Diversity

- Celebrate diversity.

- Recognize that diverse experiences drive innovations.

- Confront issues directly to understand perspectives and identify threats and opportunities.

- Stay open-minded.

Seek Mutual Benefit

- Build strong relationships.

- Focus on concrete, common goals.

- Encourage resolving conflicts for mutual benefit.

Empower

- Structure forums and settings to express ideas and frustrations.

- Foster self-confidence.

- Provide skill training.

Take Stock

• Seek feedback on how conflicts are managed.

• Celebrate successes.

• Plan for ongoing improvement.

The Costs of Poorly Managed Conflict

Perhaps the most dramatic evidence of the value of positive conflict is that suppressed conflict has resulted in major fiascoes. Ineffective conflict also affects the bottom-line results of many organizations as well as their decisions, culture, and morale. New research suggests how to measure the costs of conflict in dollars.

President John F. Kennedy and his advisors pressed foreign-policy experts to suppress their reservations about the invasion of Cuba. The Bay of Pigs fiasco remains a blot on American foreign policy. Learning from this experience, Kennedy insisted on controversy in the Cuban missile crisis, and his actions still earn him high marks.[7]

Suppressed controversy contributed to the Challenger disaster early in 1986. Engineers and managers apparently did not discuss constructively their opposing views on the safety of flying the shuttle in cold weather. The explosion seconds after takeoff cost lives and crippled the American space effort. Failure to discuss opposing views is also a major contributor to commercial airplane crashes. Flight-crew members often have the information that could avert crashes, but hesitate to challenge the pilot in command.

Corporate raiders have argued that boards of directors do not have the independence, courage, and information to challenge management and, as a consequence, do not defend the rights of shareholders properly. Harold S. Geneen, former CEO of ITT, argued that boards are unable to protect stockholders and seldom act until the company is near ruin. Investors, raiders, and managers are working to make boards more assertive.

The costs of poorly managed conflict are not limited to disasters or the boardroom. Every day employees avoid discussing their frustrations directly with their boss and continue to work in unproductive ways. Managers find it prudent to pretend to agree, withhold information, and fail to challenge inadequate decisions. Alternatively, they badger, fight, and build coalitions to get their position accepted to make themselves look good. The more powerful, cunning, and persistent win, but their decisions may still be wrong.

The costs of conflict can be put in dollar terms. Janz and Tjosvold[8] interviewed managers and employees in an engineering firm to identify specific ways that they mishandled conflicts and relationships on the job. Employees in this firm refused to communicate directly with other people, ignored advice and suggestions, did not learn from more experienced employees, viewed problems just from their own point of view, involved only those that supported their own position, embarrassed and blamed others, and let design flaws remain to make others look bad.

Managers then indicated the employee time, materials, and project days lost because the conflicts were managed ineffectively rather than effectively. These estimates suggest that destructive conflict cost the company $12,000 a year per employee in time and materials, and $30,000 if project days lost were taken into account. These results are estimates and will vary depending on the company. However, they demonstrate that the failure to manage conflict most assuredly affects the "bottom line."

The failure to manage conflict costs individual employees. Fighting tough disrupts employees' social networks and sense of security and acceptance. A lack of social support contributes to physical illness and psychological disturbance. Suppressing conflict also debilitates. Hiding and keeping frustrations and anger inside causes painful stress, which if continued induces ulcers and other stress-related disorders. People who continually avoid conflict feel powerless and unable to cope with their frustrations and problems.

Conflict, when poorly managed, costs companies and individuals. Instead of accepting conflict and using it to identify and solve problems, their failure to manage conflict becomes an additional burden. Their frustrations are compounded with a sense of failure that together sap energy and creativity that could be used to achieve organizational goals and individual aspirations.

Concluding Comments

Steve and Tom took the first steps to making Lee a conflict-positive organization. However, a conflict-positive organization requires more than a set of new words and techniques, becoming conflict-positive is an ongoing process requiring nurturance and commitment. Valuing diversity, sharing aspirations, empowering, and taking stock all contribute to positive conflict.

Current research and management experience both point to the critical value positive conflict has for companies and their people. Every employee in every organization confronts conflict and is more effective and productive when conflict is well managed. Conflict is critical for performance appraisal and strategic management, for selling hamburgers and marketing high technology, for getting ordinary and extraordinary things done. Employees need to make use of conflict, not be used by it. The next section illustrates how the positive-conflict model can help the people at Lee cope with their ongoing conflict.

References

1. E. H. Schein, *Process Consultation: Its role in Organization Development* (Reading, MA: Addison-Wesley, 1988).

2. M. Deutsch, "Fifty years of conflict." In L. Festinger (Ed.), *Retrospections on Social Psychology* (New York: Oxford University Press, 1980), pp. 46–77. M. Deutsch, *The Resolution of Conflict* (New Haven: Yale University Press, 1973). M. Deutsch, "A theory of cooperation and competition," *Human Relations* 2 (1949): 129–52. D. W. Johnson and R. T. Johnson, *Cooperation and Competition: Theory and Research* (Edina, MN: Interaction Book Company, 1989). D. W. Johnson, R. T. Johnson, K. A. Smith, and D. Tjosvold, "Pro, con, and synthesis." In B. Sheppard, M. Bazerman, and R. Lewicki (Eds.), *Research on Negotiations in Organizations* 2 (Greenwich, CT: JAI Press, 1990), pp. 139–74. D. Tjosvold, "Interdependence approach to conflict in organizations." In M. A. Rahim (Ed.), *Managing Conflict* (New York: Praeger, 1989), pp. 41–50.

3. R. R. Blake and J. S. Mouton, "Lateral conflict." In D. Tjosvold and D. W. Johnson (Eds.), *Productive Conflict Management: Perspectives for Organizations* (Minneapolis: Team Media, 1989), pp. 91–150.

4. D. Tjosvold and L. McNeely, "Innovation through communication in an educational bureaucracy," *Communication Research* 15 (1988): 568–81.

5. D. Tjosvold, "Cooperation and competition in restructuring an organization," *Canadian Journal of Administrative Sciences* (in press-a).

6. D. Tjosvold, "Making a technological innovation work: Collaboration to solve problems," *Human Relations* (in press-b).

7. I. L. Janis, *Victims of Groupthink* (Boston: Houghton Mifflin, 1972).

8. T. Janz and D. Tjosvold, "Costing effective vs. ineffective work relationships," *Canadian Journal of Administrative Sciences* 2 (1985): 43–51.

Part II

Coping with a Conflict

Conflicts that have been avoided and fought in a win-lose way, like the conflict at Lee, pose great challenges. They fuel stereotypes, suspicions, and strategies for defending and counterattacking, not the attitudes and approaches for dealing with conflicts in an open, constructive way. In addition to specific operational issues, groups and individuals fight over their relationship and how they have dealt with differences in the past. They see each other as mean, stubborn, and arrogant.

Ongoing conflict affects the dynamics within groups as well as between them. Having a common enemy can provide a unifying goal and symbol. Yet conflict can disrupt a group, especially a less-powerful group that believes it is losing. The computer people felt unappreciated and blamed, and vented some of their frustrations on each other, specifically their manager. Managing conflict between groups also involves developing within the groups the leadership and teamwork that support positive conflict.

A positive-conflict approach can begin by focusing on the dynamics between organizational groups or within them. The groups can be asked directly to identify their suspicions and ineffective ways to handle conflict and challenged to develop more productive approaches.[1] Alternatively, each group can develop more productive ways of working together and handling conflicts within their team, and then improve how they work with the antagonist group.

The consultant at Lee decided to begin by strengthening Michael's leadership and the teamwork within the computer group.

Michael and Steve were both willing to proceed this way. This approach allowed the computer group to become familiar with the idea of positive conflict, repair some of the damage to its own relationships, and regain confidence in the team and its abilities. However, this approach required the computer group to take the lead in changing the relationship with production, and the production group had to be prepared to reciprocate.

3

Breaking Out of Destructive Conflict

Where there is much desire to learn, there of necessity will be much arguing, much writing, many opinions; for opinion in good men is but knowledge in the making.
John Milton, *Doctrine and Discipline*

"Three accounting partners, very good people who discussed conflicts, yet they still broke up," Tom said to Dale as they continued to discuss the conflict program for Lee in Steve's office. "That kind of shoots a little hole in your positive-conflict idea, doesn't it?"

"The same thing happens in some marriages too," Steve said.

"People might decide to change their relationship—a manager might decide an employee needs to find another job—but the conflict could still be well discussed and managed," Dale said.

"Do you mean we can fire the whole computer group?" Steve asked jokingly.

"You could, but I doubt if you want to," Dale said. "Positive conflict means that people believe they have gained more from the conflict than they've lost. That does not mean that everyone gets what they want. If the accountants did manage their conflicts well, they probably thought that new opportunities beckoned them rather than that they were forced to get out of their present business. Presumably, they still feel good about the years they worked together."

"But sometimes one person does win and the other loses," Tom said. "Your example of firing an employee is a good one. The manager wins and the employee loses."

"It does not have to be that way," Dale said. "Dismissed employees often gain insight into their own behavior—for example, they realize that they can't just blow up on the job and insult people without paying a price. They may also realize that the job was not right for them, and they now have the incentive and opportunity to find a job they can really get fired up about. I'm not arguing that dismissing an employee is always positive, just that if it is well managed it is more likely that both the manager and the employee can gain something and as a consequence feel less like losers."

"In which case, the fired employee does less bad-mouthing of the company and manager," Steve said. "I'm getting a better feel for what you mean by positive conflict, but perhaps we should get down to what you're going to do here."

"There are a number of places that we could begin," Dale said. "Tom indicated that you wanted to begin with Michael, and he seemed quite willing when I talked with him. Michael and I would first work on how positive conflict applies to his leadership. We would discuss current ideas about being an effective leader who employs a team approach and uses conflict. Michael's very bright and well trained technically, but needs to improve his way of working with other people."

"We've talked about that," Steve said. "I suggested that he attend seminars where he could get a better understanding of his management style."

"It's important," Tom added, "that you just don't talk about ideas. He can talk...it's the doing that's important."

"Good point," Dale said. "I agree that we want to talk about specific cases of what has happened and also to plan how to approach present and future leadership cases. But it's important that he has useful guides for planning how to deal with situations."

"Okay, but you must remember that he's smart and verbal, but getting him to change how he works with others has been very difficult, at least the ways that I've used," Tom said.

"One thing that I want to emphasize is that we don't want this program to come across as implying that Michael's the problem, or that the problem lies with the computer group," Dale said. "It's everyone's problem, and we need everyone to solve it. We are beginning with Michael and his group, but we're not ending there."

"I appreciate that," Steve said. "I can see that production is part of it. In fact, I think it is part of the whole operation, even into corporate headquarters...even into my office."

"What we want to do is tell Michael that this is an opportunity for him and his group to take the first step, but that it's not just their problem to solve," Dale argued.

"Sounds good," Tom said.

"Then I would move quickly into Phase 2 of involving the computer group," Dale continued.

"I don't want to be too picky," Tom interrupted, "but I think it's important that you understand that Michael's not going to change easily." Tom was willing to get expert assistance, but he still felt that he had a good handle on the problem and could sense what would and what would not solve the problem. He thought that the solution would have to be strong and firm.

"I can believe that," Dale said. "The two of you, and Michael too, have been trying to change his leadership for some time. If there were an easy way, you would have probably already found it."

"We only claim to have tried," Steve said, and his face broke into a broad smile as he looked at Tom. "Other people might have been able to bring more finesse to the issue."

"It may sound strange to you," Dale said, "But it's easier to change a group than an individual. Michael will practice and strengthen his leadership skills as he works with the computer group. He can't be a leader and have positive conflict all by himself."

"He tries...," Tom said, laughingly. "I guess some of my frustrations are showing."

"The third part involves actually approaching the users and convincing them that the computer group wants to serve them well," Dale said. "The idea is that Michael and the computer group have begun to iron out their differences and are learning to manage conflicts within their team. They are then in a better position to approach the users, establish good relations, and manage conflict. They will be a stronger team, and they will understand the ideas and have more confidence that they can manage their conflicts with users because they have done so with each other."

"How about motivation?" Steve wondered.

"Michael, I think, realizes that the attitudes of the users gets in his way, and has even resulted in curtailing his responsibilities in the company," Dale said. "Serving clients is a strong theme for contemporary computer professionals. I expect the group will be motivated."

"I am not so sure about the computer group," Tom said. "I am not sure that they really see their role as serving."

"We can talk about that with the group so that they can see why it is important for them," Dale offered.

"I think the computer group wants to be helpful," Steve said. "I think your frustrations are showing, Tom."

"As we discussed earlier, I don't find motivation a big problem in managing conflict," Dale argued. "We want to let Michael and the computer group know why managing conflict is important to them and to the company. We're not just managing conflicts because it sounds good. In conflict that has dragged on, people are suffering, they are angry and frustrated, and feel self-righteous and guilty at the same time. They know that the conflict costs a great deal. They very much want to do something about it and often blame themselves for not doing anything."

"I think everyone is fed up," Tom said. "It's really been going on for so long. The problem is that there's a sense that not much can be done."

"People often feel the problem is bigger than them and they can't do much about it...they feel powerless," Dale said. "They're right in a way. Individually, it is very difficult to change how conflicts are managed. We need to get everyone involved so that they all work to break down the barriers together."

"How do you overcome that sense that nothing can be done?" Tom asked.

"One step at a time," Dale said. "I believe in the slow, steady approach. The way of dealing with conflicts has developed over time, it's not going to change overnight. I will encourage Michael and the computer group to take the first steps, break the counterproductive cycles, and develop the attitudes and relationships that will allow them to use their conflict skills to work productively."

"I know you can't guarantee success," Steve said. "But it would be great for the company and for Michael if we could work this out. Don't worry about running out of work. We've got other conflicts that need attention."

"I won't promise hugs and kisses," Dale said. "A successful program depends on everyone being willing to get involved and work for a solution. But I don't see any reason why we can't make progress."

"If you aren't getting anywhere, we should talk," Steve said. "No use banging heads against a wall. If you think I'm part of the problem, please come in and tell me."

"I appreciate your openness, and look forward to working with you and your people," Dale said.

Getting Organized

Dale wanted Steve, Tom, and others at Lee to understand the positive-conflict model and to see it as a realistic ideal for them to work toward. Positive conflict would also guide the process of changing the conflict and the organization. Dale wanted to use and demonstrate positive conflict in his work at Lee.

Through reading and discussion, Steve and Tom were getting a better understanding of positive conflict. It does not assume that there are no problems or conflicts or that everyone gets whatever they want. It does assert that conflict can be very useful.

Indeed, the fighting and complaints between the production and computer groups had made Tom and Steve aware and motivated to address the issues. They were open to having an outside consultant develop and carry out a plan for improving the relationship between the computer group and its users. Yet they had misgivings. In the back of their minds, they felt they had somehow failed as managers. Couldn't they, shouldn't they, have done something about this conflict years ago?

Steve and Tom confronted Dale directly with the sense of powerlessness experienced by the people at Lee. The failures of their attempts to solve the conflict and their frustrations had demoralized them. They were skeptical that much could be done.

The managers and employees at Lee had to see that positive conflict was a realistic goal for them before they would exert the effort and take the risks needed to change. Dale conveyed his own confidence that they could overcome the conflict. He wanted them to have realistic hope and to restore their confidence that they could take charge of the conflict. At the same time, Dale did not want to give substance to false expectations that there was a quick fix, such as "straightening out" Michael. Ongoing, destructive conflict is grounded in and part of more general dynamics within the organization. They could break out of the destructive conflict, but not without effort.

Dale was genuinely hopeful. Top management was addressing the issue directly; the production and computer groups admitted the problem needed attention. Openness is the first, essential step in dealing with conflict. People are getting the issues out on the table and realizing they need to deal with the conflict, even if they are not talking to each other. The consultant's role is to promote direct discussions, emphasize shared aspirations, and develop forums and skills to discuss the conflict productively. However, if people won't admit there is a conflict, the consultant has the additional, and sometimes very difficult, task of encouraging people to talk about feelings they are reluctant to reveal.

Positive conflict also suggested how Dale could work with Steve, Tom, and others at Lee. Tom, very much sensing and being part of production's frustrations with Michael, had reservations about Dale's program. He thought that it was too optimistic about Michael's openness and motivation and that it relied too much on theory. Dale recognized Tom's point of view and accepted Tom's emphasis on discussing specific cases. Dale also made it explicit that the program should not be based on the assumption that Michael and the computer group were the culprits. In addition to helping to understand and develop the program, the conflict made them all more aware of the depth of Tom's frustrations.

Although Steve, Tom, and Dale made use of their conflicts, complete openness was not present, and perhaps not needed. Dale wondered how committed Tom was to resolving the conflict. Would a respected Michael be too much of a threat to his management of the plant? Dale thought that Tom might be a part of the problem, and might be unintentionally fueling the conflict between production and management. Yet Dale realized that these were only suspicions and avoided a direct discussion of them. He wanted to wait until he had more evidence and had developed a good relationship with Tom. Conflict management does not simply mean openly discussing all issues and problems. It requires open discussion skillfully and appropriately carried out.

Working with Michael

Michael and Dale began the program the next week. Dale explained the plan to work with Michael on leadership, the computer group as a team, and reaching out to the users. Dale emphasized that the program was not based on the assumption that Michael or the computer group was at fault, only that they had the opportunity to begin to change how the computer group and its users worked together.

"I see myself working for Steve and Tom, but I am also working for you, for the computer group, for the users, for everyone here at Lee," Dale said.

"Heaven knows we can all use some help."

"Do you think that the program might be useful to you?" Dale asked.

"I sure hope it can," Michael responded. "We in the computer group get dumped on a lot. What you must understand and what really gets me is that we have worked hard over the years to make the system more reliable. And I have the evidence that the computer is much, much better. We used to make about 400,000 tons of cement a year. Last year we made over twice that. It could not have been done without big improvements in the computer. But all we get is complaints and criticisms."

"Getting the computer group more appreciated and valued by the users, I think, should be one of our major goals."

"I don't care if they like me or not; I don't think that's the issue. It is knowing what the computer has done for them."

"But isn't it important that the others respect you and your group, recognize your efforts, and support your efforts to computerize the company?"

"That's true. Okay, I can see where we want them to appreciate us."

"I see our working together as an opportunity to have you think about and develop your own leadership skills," Dale added.

"I want to," Michael said. "I've talked to Steve about taking management seminars. This program may be the way for me to become a better manager."

"I'm glad you want to improve your management skills."

"Definitely. My future, I think, is managing technology. There are more and more people who know about computers, but there is a growing need for people to manage those people. I'm not sure that there is that kind of future in Lee, but I see that as my future."

Dale agreed that there's a need for managers of technology. He also wanted to let Michael know that it was okay to talk about leaving Lee. Dale's job was not to enforce Lee's rules and values on Michael, but to develop his competence. To do this, Michael and he had to be candid.

"I think we can learn some very useful things about managing that can help you wherever you are," Dale said. "What I see us doing today is discussing ideas about managing and conflict and then next week talking about specific cases. How does that sound?"

"Good," Michael responded. "But changing things is not going to be easy. I read those articles you sent about positive conflict, but Lee does not really work the way you suggest. There is a lot of in-fighting and politics that go on in this place."

"Steve and Tom seem to be telling me that too. They realize, I think, that there are plant- and corporate-wide problems in dealing with conflict and having people work together."

"They know. They're not treated so well by their bosses. It all starts at the top."

"The top does have a lot of impact. But we should try to see how you, the computer group, and the users can cope best within Lee."

"We can do better," Michael said.

To emphasize shared aspirations and cooperative goals for the conflicts between Michael, his group, and the production department, Dale argued that it's joint work and problem solving that counts in organizations. It is through working together that information is exchanged, problems are identified and solved. The traditional idea that an organization is made up of individuals doing their own thing is very unrealistic. Trying to solve problems alone is usually quicksand that gets people in trouble. Because of the great need to work together, there are inevitably conflicts and frustrations. It is unrealistic to expect everyone to work in perfect harmony, so it is critical to manage conflict. Conflicts that are well handled help people to find more effective ways of working together and getting things done.

"The articles make sense to me," Michael said. "I don't want to be defensive, but I think I already do work with other people well.

What I don't think, though, is that we're all equal. The idea that everyone should come together about every problem and everyone has equal say, I don't buy."

"I agree that not everyone has equal knowledge. But for important issues you're going to get better solutions when everyone has a chance to put their ideas forth. We are not talking about having a vote to see who wins, or to have the manager declare himself the winner. The idea is to get the best solution possible."

"Okay. But I have trouble with that article on computers serving their customers better. I don't want us to be little patsies who have to answer to their every whim."

"It should be a two-way street. I'm not talking about giving in and being walked all over. I'm talking about dealing with conflicts openly and constructively."

Michael and Dale talked for some time on the value of working together and managing conflict in dealing with subordinates, users, and bosses. They agreed to meet the following week.

At the next session, they reiterated the value of leadership skills and of developing a strong computer team for Michael and Lee. Dale wanted Michael to be well aware of how he could benefit from the program. Leadership and teamwork were not just nice-sounding words, and skills in these areas could be very valuable for Michael.

"Let's get more specific about these ideas by taking an example of working with the users."

"Something specific...I can tell you about Greg O'Conner and the maintenance group. Those guys are crybabies, really. I sat down and went over and over what they wanted. Then we broke our backs developing the system. What happens? Greg lets the guys working for him sabotage the system. The basic problem here is authority."

"I don't understand."

"You can talk and talk to these people, but when you have the program done, then either I or the department head should have the authority to implement the system. Greg doesn't follow through with his part of the bargain. He's got to tell his people to use the system rather than gripe about it."

"So you did talk to the users before you devised the system?" Dale asked.

"Me personally, I spent hours listening to those people and asking if this is really what you want. Then we gave them what they wanted. Now they come back and say we want this and we want that. They want to change the whole system. They don't realize we spent hours and hours developing it, and you can't just start changing it like that."

"What does Greg do?"

"Nothing. He doesn't defend us, he just says to his people, 'Yes, we need that kind of computer assistance. But you know how unresponsive the computer group is.' That really burns me."

"I can see how you feel that the users are ungrateful."

"Then they can't figure out why we don't walk around with smiles on our faces. They want us to be their little errand boys and jump at their every whim."

"This example, and some other things we talked about earlier, make me think that the users don't feel it is 'their' solution. It is like you are the experts who come in to solve their problem. If you don't do it, then they're upset."

"What do you mean?" Michael asked.

"Well, it's like you give them the impression that you will solve the problem by yourself. As if the problem is 'yours,' and not 'ours.'"

"We are the experts."

"You're the experts about computers, but they're the experts about maintenance or production. It's like the users come with a problem...a monkey on their back, they throw it on your back, and you throw your solution back. Lo and behold, the solution isn't just what they wanted. There's a good chance they don't even know exactly what they want, but when you give them a solution, they know they don't want."

"Umm..."

"Even if you do solve the problem for them, they don't understand it well, they don't appreciate why there are limitations."

"But my job is to solve computer problems for people at Lee. That's why they pay me."

"What I'm saying is that you want to solve the problem with them. It's how are we going to work together to solve *our* problem, not how *you* are going to solve *their* problem."

For the next two hours, Michael described specific examples of how he worked with corporate officials and with people in the computer group.

Dale summarized, "You seem to be the kind of manager who takes a great deal of satisfaction from solving problems. I've worked with many bright people with a high degree of technological training who really like to dig in and find solutions. That's great, but remember, in an organization it's joint problem solving that counts."

"Of course, but I was working and talking with these people. We met for hours."

"Let's take the issue you just described of getting the plant a new host computer. You knew that you needed a new host computer, but when the head of information systems at corporate office balked, you went around and over him to get the computer. You got what you wanted, but he wasn't part of the solution. You may have made him look bad. He's not going to be too grateful."

"No, he wasn't. But we got what I wanted."

"Partly. You got the computer, but you also wanted the people at Lee to appreciate and value you and the computer group."

"That's true. We didn't get the credit we deserved."

"I see the same pattern in your working with the computer group on projects. You decide how to divide up the work, and then you give directions."

"Isn't that what a manager is supposed to do?"

"The manager wants an effective, fair way to distribute work, but that does not mean the manager has to do it all alone. Even if your solution is the best, your employees may not believe it is the best. They may not understand it. That can demoralize them because they don't think they are really working as productively as possible."

"Yes, but I have the big picture."

"True, but they have the little pictures. They know their own situation, their own jobs, and other specifics."

"I think I get it. You think we can make better decisions by hashing things out together."

"Not only smarter decisions, but ones that people understand and feel that they have made together. That's when they are going to be committed and energetic."

"I think I see."

"You've set yourself apart from the others. You have set yourself up for being blamed if it doesn't work out. It is not 'we' who succeed or did not, but potentially 'us vs. them.'"

"I can see it. I can be a hero if I do solve the problem, but I can be the scapegoat if the solution isn't just so."

"I think it would be easy to feel betrayed. You've worked hard to solve their problem, but instead of cheering, you hear griping."

"That's where all the conflict comes in."

"It's more than conflict, it's poorly managed, win-lose conflict. You and the users are attacking, feeling wronged, and unfairly blamed. People are angry, ready to get back, and prove they're right."

"We're touchy and ready to bite each other."

"Good old self-righteousness."

"Beautiful in all its forms," Michael said with a smile.

Reflection on Working with Michael

Dale wanted Michael to understand in specific, clear terms how the conflict-positive program would be useful to him. Michael could improve his leadership and management skills, and strengthen his own and his group's position in Lee. Dale was acting much like a process consultant in that the program was not being done to Michael as much as with and for him.[2] Without this understanding, Michael could easily feel the program was being pushed on him and that it would signify that the problems were his alone. To his credit, Michael saw that his inability to deal with people and manage conflicts well was getting in his way, and he was open to examining his problems and improving his people skills.

Dale and Michael used positive conflict as a common way to analyze Michael's leadership and style of working with others. They inevitably had different views about how Michael worked with others and opposing recommendations about what he should do. *The idea of positive conflict provided a common framework and ideal so that Dale and Michael could openly and usefully discuss their at-times opposing views.*

With this joint understanding, Dale felt that he could directly confront Michael about his tendency to solve problems by himself and then respond to Michael's counterarguments. Michael was better equipped to understand the feedback about how he worked with other people and to appreciate the strengths and limitations of his approach. Michael was not caught off-guard and was open to this confrontation because he realized that Dale was not arbitrarily blaming and scolding him. Dale was using ideas that Michael accepted to examine and improve Michael's style.

Their discussion revealed how self-sealing the conflict had become. Michael's idea that he was the expert and should solve problems had contributed to the conflict with production. However, the way the conflict was handled only reinforced his approach. He worked even harder to show that he, and not the production people or others in the computer group, had the necessary technical expertise to develop and keep the systems operating. He complained that he needed more authority to impose solutions. These attitudes fueled the conflict with production. Michael's adopting a "we" approach to leading and working with others would contribute to conflict managing.

Concluding Comments

Dale was working to establish a climate and a relationship with Michael that would permit a useful dialogue, including constructive conflict. *Learning to manage conflicts well was the thrust of the program; managing conflict was an important means to get there.* To establish this cooperative climate for conflict, Michael came to see for himself that the program would promote his own interests as well as those of the company. He and Dale had the common, valued goal of improving conflict management.

Michael was appreciating how central working with other people and dealing with their attitudes and feelings was to being a manager and to facilitating computerization at Lee. Wishing for harmony and agreement is unrealistic. He was learning that there is no real alternative to managing conflicts well. He would find these insights useful as he began to deal with the conflicts within the computer team and with the users.

References

1. R. Beckhard, "The confrontation meeting," *Harvard Business Review* 45 (1967), 149–55.
2. E. Schein, *Process Consultation: Its Role in Organization Development* (Reading, MA: Addision-Wesley, 1988).

4

Forging Links

I dogmatize and am contradicted, and in this conflict of opinions and sentiments I find delight.
Samuel Johnson

Though it was not clear from his expression—it would only become clear later through his actions—Michael was ready for the team meeting held at a hotel near the cement mill. He had developed some confidence in Dale, and while he thought a transformation of work at Lee unlikely, he recognized that a "we" approach was needed to get things done and change attitudes. He had few fears and expected the session to move the group along.

Glenda, Dick, and Sheldon welcomed the break away from the daily grind and hoped that the session would begin to lift the monkey from their backs. Yet they had forebodings, and Michael's cool demeanor did not, as it did not in many other situations, allay their apprehensions. Despite Dale's briefing, they did not have a good feel for what might happen. Sheldon doubted Michael's sincerity in developing a team approach, and he was not alone in his suspicions. Might he not say things that would haunt him and sour his relationship with Michael even more?

Dale had his own apprehensions. He had worked to get the group ready, but knew that any success would depend upon Michael and the others making use of the opportunities. He could not control how they would respond. Yet he was confident he would not ask them to do things they were unprepared or unable to do. He enjoyed the anticipation, and knew he would learn more about the people and their group.

"Welcome to our first annual Lee Computer Team Development Day," Dale said with tongue-in-check gusto. "It will be a day filled with excitement and memories."

Michael broke into a smile, and Sheldon retorted, "I wonder if we will remember Dale at our second annual meeting."

The humor took some edge off the apprehensions, and emphasized the positive side of working together. Dale enjoyed teasing, but did not want the session to degenerate into one-liners and oneupmanship. There was work to be done, and there were conflicts to manage.

"We do have important goals for today," Dale continued. "As I've discussed before, Michael and I thought it would be useful to look at what kind of team we want to be and to become more aware of the skills and abilities we have to become that team. We all know our mission and each other, but we thought it would be useful to refocus on our common hopes and the very real resources we have in the group. Later we will look at the barriers and problems that get in our way."

Dale then set up a group problem solving experience. They took the roles of the local police who wanted to solve a murder mystery.[1] The clues to identify the murderer, motive, and time were distributed to all team members. They were told that they, working as a group, should find the best solution to the problem. They were all eager problem solvers, and through fits and starts found ways to develop the correct answer.

Dale asked them to reflect on their working together on a common project. They talked about how collaborating was fun and exhilarating, but not simple. They had to find ways to exchange and summarize their information. They had to deal with conflict because they pointed out shortcomings in each other's logic and reasoning. Everyone's ideas had to be challenged and revised. They realized there is a richness and complexity to making a team work, but there are also great rewards. As Michael summarized, "We couldn't do it by ourselves, and it was fun to get everyone's ideas. It brought home a good point about working together." The theme of the demands and rewards of teamwork would be repeated throughout the day.

To focus on the computer group's cooperative goals and shared aspirations, each person described the kind of team that he or she wanted their group to become. Michael emphasized that he wanted a team that created a reliable, accurate computer system that was cost effective, neat, and professional. He wanted the group to be cohesive and to present a unified front to the users. The group should be valuable and be seen as valuable by the users. He hoped that individuals would have challenging, rewarding jobs, and said that he as the leader needed to be kept informed.

Sheldon followed with similar themes. He wanted the group to give good service to the users, to understand their point of view, and to earn their respect. He hoped the group would improve its communication and that the group members would know what each other was doing and be friendlier and more relaxed with each other. The individuals should be treated as professionals, given more autonomy, and have opportunities to attend seminars.

Glenda and Dick had similar hopes for their group. Dick wanted less crisis management with the users. The team should help the users learn how to solve problems rather than be dependent on them for solutions. Glenda was interested in getting more involved with the process computers. She looked forward to working face-to-face with the production people and getting more hands-on experience.

The computer group found a great deal of overlap in the kind of team they wanted. They summarized their views as wanting a computer group who knew the users well and took their perspective; they wanted to be appreciated as valuable and respected by the users. They needed to show the users that they were on their side, and on the same team. The team should nurture their own professional development so that they could keep abreast of the fast-changing technology and enhance the computer capabilities and culture of Lee. Finally, and most importantly, they realized that they had to work together. They needed to know each other's agendas, brainstorm ideas, and be united.

"Now I will put you to work. I want you to write down all your strengths, abilities, and successes that can help you contribute to the computer group's becoming the kind of team you want," Dale said. Dale wanted them to feel empowered to become an effective team that could manage its conflicts.

"Give us something easy," Dick teased. "Let's talk about our weaknesses. The company goes to great measures to make sure we are well aware of what we do wrong."

Each team member in turn identified his or her abilities, and other team members reinforced and added ones not mentioned.

Team members quickly overcame modesty and directly announced their own and others' strengths. They became more fully aware that they had important skills within their own team, and they deserved to be confident they could create the team they wanted.

Their abilities were highly complementary. Glenda was confident she could work well with individual users. She had a natural patience and did not mind carefully explaining how they could make the computer work. The users tended to be more restrained with her as a woman. Dick had already established good communication links and often ate lunch with the users. He had good, practical hardware skills. Michael had the overall view of how the computer system had developed and where it was headed at Lee. He also had over a decade of experience working within the larger corporate structure. He protected and worked for his group in the political climate of the corporation. Sheldon had a strong user orientation and great deal of experience in user-needs analysis from his previous job. Also, when he brought his dogs out to the plant on weekends to run in the nearby open areas, he had opportunities to enjoy small talk with a number of users and to develop an affinity that carried to the workplace.

The group began to "gossip" about individual users of the computer system. It turned out that while they shared a common wariness of the production group, their experiences with individuals were very different. The nasty, mean user to one was an understandable, sympathetic character to another. For example, Sheldon said he thought Ken Landers was just a grumpy, foul-mouthed nay sayer. Michael responded, without harshness, that he had gotten to know Ken as a person. He gave Ken a ride home after a company party several years ago, and Ken, who had had a few drinks, talked about his crippled, pain-ridden child and the wife that had deserted them. Michael understood why Ken did not go around with a smile on his face. The team began to realize that it was the people they did not know that they would dismiss as ungrateful, spiteful people.

It was evident that together they were much stronger than alone. Together they had the abilities to become the kind of team they envisioned and had the relationships with the users they needed to be successful. And Michael demonstrated his commitment to a team approach.

Michael and Sheldon

After lunch, Dale distributed the results of a questionnaire they had completed. The findings indicated they were united in their ideal of a team with strong common goals that shares information willingly, faces conflict openly, and expresses opposing views. Reality fell far short. What surprised them was that they felt more effective in the way they worked with Michael than with each other. Michael was surprised that there was general agreement on how they worked with him; he tended to think that Sheldon was much more negative than the others. Not surprisingly, they felt they had greater shortcomings with the users than with each other or with Michael.

Dale wanted them to confront specific conflicts to get a better understanding of the barriers before them. Sheldon, the bravest and most frustrated, began. He talked about the need for meetings to discuss issues and brainstorm what could be done. Then he directed his attention to Michael.

"Well, I guess it is up to me to get this going. I think we have to look at the kind of leadership we get. As a simple thing, Michael, you have us work in Cobol, and no self-respecting computer professional works with that any more." Sheldon looked at Michael, who smiled wanly, looked down, and took notes. Sheldon continued. "What I find frustrating, Michael, is that you begin a program and then we have to complete it. But you know how individual programming is. I would rather do the work from the beginning." Sheldon looked up again, saw Michael writing notes, and continued. "We are too much like your appendages—you assign us tasks, but we don't know how others are doing."

Consistent with his respectful, methodological style, Michael responded to each of Sheldon's points. "I agree Cobol is a dinosaur, and I wouldn't ask you to do it except that is what we are stuck with, at least for a while until we get the new technology I have been pressing for. It's a struggle to bring this company up to date. I hope too that someday we can say good riddance to Cobol." Michael looked at his notes. "I have no problem trying to think of new ways of getting the work organized." Michael and Sheldon began to brainstorm how they might construct and assign tasks more effectively and together. It was a beginning.

Michael signaled his openness and sincerity, and challenged Sheldon's long-held assumptions about him. The confrontation fostered confidence and trust, which in turn began to open up daily communication that would serve Glenda and Dick as well as Michael and Sheldon.

The team wanted to put their new sense of team to work, and they made several changes. They decided to have morning meetings to touch base, share pressing problems, and make sure they knew what each was doing. In this way, they felt more involved and more like a team; they also appeared more united to the users, because they knew what each other was doing. They also began bi-weekly brainstorming sessions. People would know before the meeting what the topic was, such as a project one of them was working on or a large project that the group wanted to begin, and together would hammer out how they should begin. They were becoming an energetic team.

Building a Team

The conflict-positive framework guided efforts to repair the damaged relations within the computer group and laid the foundation for direct confrontation with production. The ongoing conflict had undercut the computer group's morale and unity. The team felt divided and powerless.

The program was to engender strong feelings of *seeking mutual benefit and cooperative aspirations*. It worked to *empower* the computer people by giving them confidence that they had the abilities and the wherewithal to be successful, and taught them to *take stock* of themselves and identify specific issues. Then the team would be more prepared to confront specific differences and to *value their diversity*.

Michael, Sheldon, Glenda, and Dick knew they shared the task of providing computer services and belonged to the same administrative group, but their conflicts had split them apart. What unity they did have was based too much on hostility and defensiveness toward users. They responded as a team when attacked by the users, though here too they would try to dissociate themselves and blame others. This "hate our common enemy" was a shaky basis on which to build a team.

Discussing their visions for the team reinforced the fact that they had shared aspirations and had much to gain through collaboration. Indeed, the team was essential if the individuals were going to get what they wanted. Their mutual interests became concrete and motivating. Their joint vision, they saw, was related to their own needs and aspirations.

This sense of unity helped them feel more powerful. They collectively identified abilities and strengths that they could apply to solving problems and getting things done. Reflecting on the results of their questionnaires clarified and made public that they had work to do to strengthen their relationships. Working on their shared vision and empowering did not negate conflict, but gave it a new, powerful meaning.

Beginning to Conflict

Sheldon and Michael's discussion helped the computer team strengthen its conflict capabilities. The team saw in concrete, personal terms that conflict was a natural, inevitable aspect of working together and that by dealing with it team members could realize their personal and common aspirations. Rather than fear or mistrust conflict, they could use it to move forward.

In addition to that day's team building, groundwork for the conflict had been previously laid. Dale and Michael discussed the results of the questionnaire that indicated that the three team members worked with Michael in similar ways. This feedback challenged Michael's assumption that Sheldon was a "rotten apple" spoiling teamwork. Dale reminded Michael that outspoken people often brought issues and information out so that problems could be addressed. Michael did not want to blame the messenger for the message, and even more, he did not want to hide from the message.

Sheldon was also beginning to rethink some of his assumptions about Michael. In a prior interview, Sheldon had argued that Michael was all-powerful and got whatever he wanted from the corporation. Dale told him that Michael had had many battles with corporate officers and felt quite frustrated. Dale argued that, in contrast to Sheldon's portrait, he thought Michael was open to new ways of working and interested in protecting and assisting those who worked for him. Dale asked Sheldon to be open to reassessing his conclusions about Michael's closed-mindedness and not to dismiss Michael's efforts prematurely.

This groundwork was useful, but it was Michael and Sheldon who had to discuss their conflicts productively. They took the risks and confronted their difficulties head on. They discovered that this openness was not that difficult, and that they could draw upon their own skills. The success they had was theirs.

Dale could have asked Michael and Sheldon for a face-to-face discussion about their conflict without such preparation. If handled well, the discussion could have sparked considerable progress and been a more efficient way to proceed. However, such confrontations can be very taxing and can identify so many issues that the participants are overwhelmed. Repairing their damaged relationship and clarifying misconceptions and suspicions before a direct discussion, while more time consuming, helped them manage their conflict.

Approaching Production

The team session underlined for the members of the computer group the need for them to develop productive relationships with their "customers," the production group. At a morning session, Dale asked them to focus on how they could approach the users. First, they indicated how they thought the users viewed them. The computer group believed that the users were highly critical of them. Production employees, they thought, wanted little to do with them and saw them as fat, lazy, and uncaring.

Dale then summarized his interviews with the users. The users were frustrated, but realized that the computer group was vital; they felt very vulnerable and highly dependent upon the computer group. The computer group were nice people who would help, but sadly didn't think much of, nor like, the users. The users did not like being so tough on the computer group on occasion, but explained they were under much more pressure than the computer group appreciated. The computer group, they thought, overpromised and probably did not have sufficient resources. They felt guilty because they had withdrawn and let things slide rather than face issues directly.

The users' views shook the computer group's assumptions. Dale did not press them to accept his summary, but challenged them to remain open to revising their assumptions about the users.

"Dale, you have been talking to us about managing our conflicts and working with the users," Sheldon said. "Sounds good, but why is all this so one sided? How come it is always us that are supposed to change and do things differently? You've told us that it takes two to have a conflict and two to manage it, but now it's like we have to do it all ourselves. It all seems so contradictory, and it's not fair."

"I'm glad you are getting more comfortable dealing with conflict...I guess I'm glad," Dale replied. "Seriously, we have a harmful cycle here where one side blames and attacks the other and then the other counterattacks, which provokes another attack, and so on. Each side feels wronged. Someone has to break the cycle. You have the opportunity, the challenge, and the possibility of taking the first step."

"What's in it for us?" Dick asked. "You should see all the abuse I have taken over the years. Now you want us to lay over and play dead like pansies." Dick's anger, built up over the years, quickly surfaced.

"I'm not talking about being pushovers," Dale said. "We are talking managing conflict here, not giving in and giving up. You have a lot to gain by having good links with the users. I think you'll be proud that it was you who took the first step. I think the users will appreciate that as well." Dale knew that he had not convinced them, but they were willing to consider the position, and it helped them to feel that the course was not unreasonable.

Brainstorming

The team brainstormed what they could do to make their first steps successful and get the users to reciprocate. They developed a number of possibilities. First, they wanted to strengthen their own team, and continue to communicate openly and manage conflicts. This would help them feel more confident and skillful. Being strong and united would help them deal with the users of the computer system.

Then they wanted to refine their skills in managing conflict. They could practice using the ideas and guidelines that they had discussed and read. In particular, they thought that they needed to know how to handle highly agitated people. A production person would storm in shouting and angry about the computer or what she thought was a computer problem, and the programmer would get upset and defensive and try to show that it was not the computer but the production person's own lack of knowledge. These incidents kept the bad feelings alive and intense. Dale liked the ideas and agreed to plan a session that included how "not to let your button be pushed."

The most difficult issue was to decide how to approach users directly. How could they tell the users in practical, credible ways that they wanted a more open, cooperative way of dealing with problems and conflicts? They thought breakfast or lunch meetings would signal this intent and provide a chance to talk to the workers as individuals. Dale suggested that they could make a video in which they spoofed themselves and the old way of working with users. He argued that it would be a fun way of telling the users that the computer group understood their feelings and how the computer group sometimes came across.

In the end, the computer group decided against such meetings and videos. It was probably more practical to meet with the top supervisors, show them that they wanted to work together with them, and begin projects in which they demonstrated very specifically that they wanted a more cooperative working relationship.

Meeting the Production Managers

The computer group went over their approach for the session with the production superintendent, Rick, the maintenance supervisor, Greg, and the head of the laboratory, Loren Hill, who was also the assistant production superintendent. They wanted to show the users that they were trying to develop better relationships in which they understood and responded to the users' concerns. They wanted the managers to get the word to their employees that there was a new relationship being worked out in which they were to work with the computer group.

Rick, because of his position and the force of his personality, set the tone. He appeared to be a simple man, but he could be misunderstood. His large stature, lack of formal education, deep voice, and reputation for getting angry made him easy to stereotype. But, as Dale was learning and Michael already knew, Rick's tough, demanding outward demeanor obscured the fact that he was a sensitive, caring man who took his responsibilities to make cement and take care of his people very seriously. In his interview with Dale, he came across as a frustrated man who wanted solutions to his problems, including the computer, but without bitterness. He wanted a relationship with the computer group that was personal and open, in which conflicts were managed.

Rick was prepared to give the computer group a good hearing, and was ready to pitch in. Greg was a sensible, practical person who realized that he had much to learn from Rick. He was willing to follow Rick. Loren was the only college graduate, but the education had not left him particularly open. He was suspicious of Michael and skeptical of any changes. He had more than a "show-me" attitude; he was ready to see the computer group fail.

Dale reminded them that the computer group wanted to develop good relationships with their users in which not everything would be rosy, but when problems and difficulties did arise, they would be able to resolve them. Rick, Greg, and Loren were asked to identify how the relationship could be improved.

After some pause, Rick said, "I can start. We could communicate better, and keep each other informed. We don't know each other as people very well, and we don't know each other's priorities." Greg added that the groups needed to find better ways of troubleshooting and problem solving. They had no way to get together to discuss issues together. Loren argued that the computer group was too remote. Rick said he wanted to feel more confident in the computer system and the group. He didn't like surprises because it meant he might be surprised in the future at the wrong time and place. He let the computer team know that having a good computer system was not enough; the users needed to feel confident and informed or else they would always worry when disaster might strike, even as the mill was going full steam.

The computer group listened, but it was hard for them not to take offense. The old patterns of feeling attacked and then counterattacking were not far from the surface.

In a crisp voice that the computer group took as harshness, Loren complained that requests of the computer group seldom got handled quickly enough and some got lost. That pushed Michael's button. He expressed his anger indirectly by talking quickly and trying to convince Loren that he was wrong. He went over the system and explained how work orders could not get lost. Loren countered. Dale tried to interrupt the pattern, but Michael just talked over him.

Then the discussion took a worse turn. Sheldon said, "Those work orders go right to Michael, and sometimes the rest of us don't even see them."

Michael took this, as others did, as an attack on his leadership and a sign of disunity. Michael stared back at Sheldon, "The work orders do not end up on my desk."

It was a time that demanded leadership and Rick came through. He listened patiently, refused to get sidetracked into such a discussion, and said, "There will always be problems. We aren't going to solve everything, but what we want is to be able to know each other better and work together to solve them. By the way, I've told my men that we shouldn't yell and shout so much with the computer group. We're looking for a better way of working." Loren got the message.

Dale asked them to focus on what they could do so that they could manage problems and conflicts more effectively. Greg said that they could meet regularly with Michael much as he does with Rick and Loren on maintenance issues. They could set priorities that fit the needs of the production, maintenance, and computer groups. The group could also identify people from these areas to form project teams to work on particular areas to make the computer system more effective and useful. Rick offered to contribute from his budget to projects that they identified as high priority but for which the computer group did not have sufficient resources.

Michael announced that people from the computer group would be attending the early morning production meeting. Production people thought their absence signaled their lack of interest in them, and their desire to sleep late. Michael also said that they wanted to spend more time with individual users. Rick liked that. "My people will like showing you what they do, and you will know better the kind of pressure they're under."

"Sounds like a beginning," Rick said. "Let's all go for lunch. Michael, you can pay," Rick said with a laugh.

Integrating the Production and Computer Groups

The computer team was chipping away at the barriers between them and the production department and other users. Progress was not dramatic, nor was it inevitable. Dale shuddered when Michael got into the old mode of arguing and showing that he was right; his heart sank when Sheldon undercut Michael at the meeting. But they recovered and continued.

After the meeting, Michael confided in Dale that he did get angry and had let Loren push his button. He was thankful that Rick helped move the session back on course. He agreed with Dale that Rick was a good person to have a fight with and a person one could deal with. Michael knew he could expect Loren to be feisty, and that made him more regretful that he got angry and stubborn.

Michael was still angry with Sheldon. Dale agreed that Michael should talk to him and let him know his feelings. "Remember, you can't expect to be perfect, nor expect Sheldon to be. What is important is dealing with the conflicts constructively." Later they did discuss the conflict.

The computer group was taking the first steps, but they were trying to change their relationship together with the users. They needed the users to appreciate their efforts and to reciprocate. They were doing it together.

Positive conflict was a realistic framework for the users and the computer team. They could focus on the pressing issues of lack of communication and trust. They did not have to achieve an ideal of smooth harmony, and did not have to feel they had failed when frustrations arose. They expected difficulties as they worked for better work relationships. Even though their meeting was not smooth, the people at the session generally had confidence that they were developing a new attitude and a commitment to work things out.

Concluding Comments

The computer group was emphasizing its cooperative goals and developing a team vision. Team members identified their strengths and abilities, examined their own dynamics, and approached some of their conflicts in an open, productive manner. With this team unity, they began to address barriers between them and their "customers." Their meeting with the users, though peppered with argument and dissent, opened up the lines of communication.

The computer group and production had begun to repair the damage of their ongoing conflict. Yet there was still much work to be done. They still needed to structure forums and methods to handle problems and differences. Indeed, they had to strengthen their work relationship or risk falling back into old patterns. They were in a better position to put positive conflict to work to help them solve problems, negotiate differences, and resolve their anger and frustrations. However, they would have to continue to take risks and experiment to use conflict productively.

References

1. D. W. Johnson and F. P. Johnson, *Joining Together: Group Theory and Group Skills* (Englewood Cliffs, NJ: Prentice-Hall, 1988).

Part III
Positive Conflict at Work

Conflict is much more than angry outbursts; managing conflict is much more than coping with crises. People debate their opposing ideas and positions as they explore problems and create decisions. They negotiate their different preferences and discuss their relationship to forge a common ground. They express and manage their frustration, anger, and dismay so that they can feel accepted by colleagues and involved in the company. Conflict can be put to use to promote an organization's effectiveness.

The failure to use conflict is costly. Problems are not understood or solved; common aspirations are lost; people feel distant and estranged from each other and the company.

Managers and employees should be prepared not only to use conflict knowledge to cope with destructive conflicts, but also to structure and encourage productive conflict. Nowhere is this more true than in solving problems. Considerable evidence indicates that making important decisions without discussing opposing views is a very risky course, which undermines the potential of collective brainstorming and judgment. Chapter 5 outlines procedures for using positive conflict to make decisions. Chapter 6 shows how negotiating can help employees focus on and achieve their common aspirations. Chapter 7 describes how a conflict-positive approach can turn anger into a powerful social force.

People at Lee had begun to repair their relationships so that they were more able to put positive conflict to work. However, they needed to use conflict to make decisions, negotiate, and deal with anger, or risk undoing their progress.

5

Making Decisions

*Since the general or prevailing opinion on any subject is
rarely or never the whole truth, it is only by the collision of
adverse opinion that the remainder of the truth has any
chance of being supplied.*
    John Stuart Mill

*Some of those terrible moves [by the Chrysler board] could
have been stopped by just one bold man asking, "Why are
we doing this? Does it really make sense?"*
    Lee Iacocca, CEO, Chrysler Corporation

Members of the computer team were in a sober mood. After
the initial enthusiasm of dealing directly with major frustrations,
they realized their problems were far from over. They had to renew
their effort to make steady, albeit slow, progress. Problems within
the organization were highly related and would not disappear
without a fight. They needed to think of chipping away at them,
getting others on board, and creating an effective team organization
over months, not days.
    Sheldon, Glenda, and Dick grumbled when Dale stopped by
to check progress. They agreed that they were better informed of
each other's directions and needs, that they felt freer to contribute,
and that communication had improved—but they were not yet a
team. The problem, they argued, was that Michael was not open. He
allowed a little discussion and input, but after they had discussed
issues briefly, Michael would look at his watch, remind them time

was almost up, and announce the solution, which was usually very close to Michael's original position.

Sheldon was the most outspoken. "Michael just does not want to give up that power. He's used to having the power and wants to get his way." Yet, pressed by Dale, they admitted that Michael at times did change his mind, but he had that "you-have-to-convince-me" attitude that made team brainstorming a struggle up a hill they were unlikely to climb.

At his next meeting with Michael, Dale asked about team brainstorming and decision making. He wanted to know Michael's feelings about specific issues the computer group had discussed. "The sessions were okay, they were useful," Michael said, after some thought. "There was not that much give and take. There is a limit to how much these people can contribute. They have fancy ideas about what we should do, but most of them are not realistic, given the anticomputer culture at Lee."

Now it was Michael's turn to complain. While the computer group may work better together and with the users, it was the same old Lee organization. "The corporation is not managed well. Everyone is looking out for their own interests, and trying to make themselves look good. Not many care about the long-term interest of the company. I wonder why I should care." Dale noted again to himself the parallel between what Michael said about his managers and what Sheldon said about Michael.

The company has never understood that computers were essential to making cement, Michael continued. He would have to justify everything by its payback and return on investment, but that missed the point of developing a computer-literate company. The company had to be dragged into using contemporary technology. Its original approach was mistaken, and he had been playing patch-up and catch-up for eight years. Instead of developing a program that was integrated and future looking, he had to get pieces here and there. In the end, the company would spend a lot more money and take longer to make the system work properly and reliably.

"You seem to be saying that top management will not let you design and develop the best computer system possible. You can't work directly for the best system, but have to get pieces here and there," Dale reflected.

"That's right. I have to break it down into parts and then try to sell each part to Steve and the corporate office, who can't think past the next quarter's profit statement. Sheldon wants us to go to a different design altogether. I am not saying he's wrong; he may well be right. However, he and the others don't know the corporate people and their thinking like I do."

"I can see why you feel forced into this piecemeal approach, but can't you take the lead and propose a long-term, integrated solution for the computer system at Lee?"

"What's the point? Why should we knock ourselves out doing that when there is so little chance they will accept it?"

"Even if the corporate office wouldn't buy the long-term approach, you may get them thinking and they may appreciate your efforts. I can also see how a good discussion would be useful for the computer team. Everyone would have a better understanding of the choices and eventual program. People would feel more involved."

"It would require a lot of time and work for little return."

"We could make it fun and exciting," Dale said. He then outlined how they could assign conflicting positions to help make the decision.

Michael was uneasy. He thought that he may be giving up some of his authority, but Dale countered that he still would have the ultimate say. The conflict would bring out and develop arguments that Michael could use. The discussion would make him more prepared and might actually improve his clout with top management. He would gain, not lose.

Michael didn't want to impose another assignment on the computer team, which had plenty of other things to do. Dale countered that he believed the team members would welcome the chance to get more involved and would benefit from understanding the political realities. They could easily see Michael as arbitrary and stubborn if he continued with the piecemeal approach without such a discussion. Michael would demonstrate openness and expose the team to the confines placed on them by the corporation.

Dale described the dynamics of positive conflict in decision making, outlined general procedures, and with Michael worked out a plan for the computer team.

Dynamics of Positive Conflict in Decision Making

Conflict, when well managed, contributes very significantly to solving problems. Decision makers need to value their diverse views and confront them directly, recognize that their goals are cooperative,

and have forums and skills to discuss their opposing ideas constructively. Many conflicts in decision making are handled poorly; discussing controversial opinions can be difficult, but, as documented by
many research studies, positive conflict can dramatically improve
the dynamics and outcomes of decision making.[1]

Elaborating

*To be persuasive we must be believable; to be believable we
must be credible; to be credible, we must be truthful.*
    Edward R. Murrow, journalist

Stay, you imperfect speakers, tell me more.
    Shakespeare, *Macbeth*

Employees as they begin to conflict over a decision elaborate
and explain their own position and ideas. The opposing positions are
related to how to solve a problem they face. Michael and Sheldon, for
example, had different views about the computer system that would
be best for Lee.

Figure 5.1
Positive Conflict in Decision Making

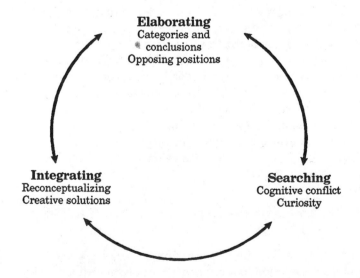

Employees identify their positions and the extent to which they are confident or have reservations about them. They list the facts, information, and theories that validate their theses, and provide a logical structure that links the facts to the conclusion. Often people appreciate their own positions, assume that their positions are superior, and want to prove that their ideas are "right" and that their position should be accepted.

As the conflict is engaged, other employees elaborate their own views, and these are often different and incompatible. The clash of opposing views interrupts any decision making and movement. Proponents may feel frustrated and argue their positions and develop their arguments more completely and forcefully. They repeat old and add new information, present more ideas, and elaborate on their positions.

Searching

Difference of opinion leads to inquiry, and inquiry to truth.
Thomas Jefferson

The opposing ideas and positions challenge each other. People critique each other's arguments, and point out weaknesses and possible strengths in the arguments. They rebut counterarguments and elaborate, but they also come to doubt the wisdom and correctness of their own position. The ideas and logic of others create internal, cognitive conflict challenging whether their original position is as useful and sensible as they had assumed.

People become uncertain about the validity of their original thesis. With this conceptual conflict, they actively search for new information. They read more relevant material, gather new information, and ask others for information. They ask their adversaries to clarify their positions and rephrase their arguments so that they can understand the opposing position more thoroughly.

Because of their curiosity, they know and remember the arguments, reasoning, and facts that support alternative positions. They can take the perspective of their opponents, anticipate how they might think about future issues, and identify the kind of reasoning they would like to employ.

Integrating

One completely overcomes only what one assimilates.
Andre Gide

The elaboration and search leaves people open-minded and knowledgeable about the issue. They have approached the issue from several perspectives, and are not rigidly fixed to their own point of view. They can synthesize and bring different ideas and facts together into a single position. They sense new patterns and new ways to integrate ideas. They incorporate others' information and reasoning into their own and develop a position responsive to several points of view. Repeated exposure to positive-conflict discussion fosters more sophisticated and higher-level reasoning and cognitive development.[2]

Consequences

These dynamics have been shown to result in high-quality, innovative solutions and agreements. The mix and clash of the discussion creates new positions not previously considered. These positions combine the arguments and perspectives of several people in elegant ways.

People are satisfied and feel they have benefited from the discussion. They enjoy the excitement, feel aroused by the challenges of the conflict, and develop positive attitudes toward the experience. They are committed to the new agreements and positions because they understand how they are related to their own interests and positions and why the adopted position is superior to their original one. Conflict then is critical for successful participation in which people "own" and feel committed to decisions.[3]

The rewards of positive conflict are rich indeed. They are much more than proving that one is right or dominant. Positive conflict is intellectually stimulating and results in effective solutions and strengthened work relationships.

_____

Using Advocacy Teams to Make Decisions

The best way ever devised for seeking the truth in any given situation is advocacy: presenting the pros and cons from different, informed points of view and digging down deep into the facts.
   Harold S. Geneen, former CEO, ITT

Managers often encourage conflict in decision making by asking everyone to speak their minds and tell it like it is. These are weak ways to structure a discussion that digs into issues. Setting up advocacy teams and assigning them different positions is a thorough way to develop constructive, conflictive discussion.

Phase 1: The manager selects a problem important enough to warrant the time and resources needed to explore it comprehensively. Then, working with others, the manager identifies the major alternative positions.

Michael and Dale recognized that developing a computer team's position on the future development of the system was highly important. The decision involved millions of dollars and would significantly affect the profitability of Lee. Through their own conflictive discussion, Michael also became convinced that developing such a proposal could well affect that decision and would have other benefits.

Phase 2: Advocacy teams are formed and each team is assigned a major alternative. They are given the time and resources to find all the supporting facts, information, evidence, and reasons for their alternative. They plan how they can present their arguments so that everyone is well aware of the strengths of their position. Their goal is not to win the debate by getting their position accepted, but they still want to present their arguments forcefully and thoroughly so that their position is seriously considered.

Michael selected Sheldon and Dick to present the position that the computer group should develop a new design, and Glenda and he would defend the present piecemeal approach. Each team had one person (Sheldon or Glenda) that was highly aware of new developments and one person (Michael or Dick) that was inclined to continue the present course and knew the corporate history. Each group would then have a range of opinions and ideas to draw upon; it would have internal conflict to help it anticipate opposing arguments and prepare its own.

Phase 3: Each team presents its arguments and position fully and persuasively; at the same time each open-mindedly listens to the other's positions. In this free discussion, they develop their own arguments, advocate their position, defend it against refutation, and counter opposing arguments. They take notes and challenge inadequate facts and reasoning. They may paraphrase each other's position and arguments to demonstrate that they have listened and understood them. Throughout the discussion, they remember that their purpose is to enable the whole group to develop as strong a position as possible.

The computer team shed its typical laid-back style and got into the debate with emotion. The teams used fancy graphics to further their arguments. Michael felt much more relaxed than normal, and showed his wit. There was an exciting tension in the air, and serious probing of alternatives.

Phase 4: A consensus decision. The teams drop their assigned position, and using all the facts and arguments identified reach a general agreement on the best course of action. They change their minds because of the logic and evidence, not because others are more powerful or argue more loudly. The decision reflects their best joint reflected judgment.

The computer team concluded that a new design would serve the company best in the long run. Their discussion indicated though that they still have a year in which to make the decision. After that, it would be increasingly expensive to shift over from the present design. The team developed a tightly reasoned report that summarized their findings.

Phase 5: Approach management and others to make and implement the decision. Making a decision in an organization is more than getting the right answer. Decisions are not puzzles to be solved; they are part of the stream of working and managing. The solution must be accepted and implemented, its impact assessed, and new problems identified.

The team's report and their solid endorsement of it gave Michael strong material to approach top management. Their decision was presented in a way that gave top management time to consider options. They had also clarified and identified the costs of the present piecemeal approach.

Even if top management decided against their recommendation, the computer team had used their time wisely. They were in a better position to anticipate the shortcomings in the present design. Moreover, the whole team understood the dilemmas and problems. If top management voted against the new system, the team would not blame Michael for failing to pursue a new design. The team members would also better understand the corporate world of Lee. They would know that they could not by themselves change Lee, but that they gave it a good try.

After the decision, the computer team met to talk about how they used conflict to make decisions. They agreed that the approach was exciting, involving, and worthwhile, but it was not an easy approach. It was tempting to fall back into the typical mode of trying to dominate and "win" by getting one's position accepted. They could easily get caught up in proving they were right and the other wrong. They had to remind themselves that what counted was *not who was right at first but that the group was right at the end.*

Advocacy Teams Guides

Phase 1: Select a problem that warrants a comprehensive evaluation. Identify the major alternative positions.

Phase 2: Assign teams opposing positions. Provide resources for teams to gather arguments and information for their position.

Phase 3: Each team presents its arguments. Others listen open-mindedly. Constructively challenge positions.

Phase 4: Members drop assigned positions. Examine all the evidence and arguments. Reach a consensus decision.

Phase 5: Approach those that can make and implement the decision.

Procedures for Conflict Decision Making

Managers have several ways to encourage conflict in decision making.

Value Diversity

1. **Heterogeneous members.** People who differ in background, expertise, opinions, outlook, and organizational position are likely to disagree. Independent thinkers and people from outside the department and organization will make controversy more likely.

2. **Openness norms.** Everyone should be encouraged to express his or her opinions, doubts, uncertainties, and hunches. Ideas should not be dismissed because they at first appear too unusual, impractical, or undeveloped.

Individual exercise of the right to dissent and free speech reduces fears of retribution for speaking out.

3. **Structure conflict.** Subgroups assigned to advocate opposing views insure open discussion of issues. A devil's advocate takes a critical evaluation role by attacking what appears to be the group's solution. Managers can actively seek to encourage various viewpoints and assure others that they are not rigidly fixed to their present position. Requiring consensus decision making encourages full participation and encourages people who have doubts to speak out. Majority vote can degenerate into attempts to get a majority and force that decision on others.

Seek Mutual Benefit

1. **An engaging, shared vision.** Decision makers are committed to their common goals and tasks. They know that their vision will promote their own values and needs as well as the company's and that they are all committed to it. Common tasks help decision makers recognize that they must work together to create the best solution. They develop their own name, distinctive character, and ways of working. Friendly, warm encounters build trust and the ability to discuss opposing views.

2. **Strive for "win-win," cooperative solutions.** Decision makers communicate expectations that they will work for a solution that benefits all. Efforts to pursue individual objectives at others' expense are discouraged. They say, "We are all in this together," and, "Let's see a solution that is good for everyone," not, "I am right, and you are wrong." Financial rewards, evaluations, and prestige are given for the group's success, not for independent work, appearing better than others, or proving that one is right. Decision makers avoid looking for winners and losers but focus on a productive solution to the common problem. Rewards are shared for success; responsibility for failure is accepted.

Empower

1. **Personal regard.** Decision makers believe they are accepted and valued as persons even though others criticize

their ideas. They listen to everyone's ideas respectfully, and criticize these ideas rather than attack an individual's motivation and personality. Insults or implications that challenge another's integrity, intelligence, and motives are avoided. Communication of interest and acceptance is accompanied by disagreement with another's current position. Demonstrating understanding by accurately paraphrasing opposing ideas is a concrete way to convey acceptance and interest in another as a person while disagreeing.

People should not confuse disagreement with their ideas as personal rejection or a rebuff. Having one's ideas challenged can be taken as a sign of interest in one's position and as a way to further one's learning. Decision makers should separate the validity of their thinking from their own competence and worth as people.

Some people find it very difficult to distinguish their self-esteem from the validity of their present position: they think they have to be right to prove themselves competent. A team approach to dealing with this issue is to have employees communicate their respect for each other and ensure that they see and value each other's strengths. At their first retreat, Michael and the computer team recognized and gave each other feedback on their resources and abilities. Team members who feel generally accepted as valued persons will feel less need to prove their value by insisting that their position is "right."

In addition, a trusted person can help individuals understand that demanding to be right is counterproductive and works against their own interests. Individual therapy is an option for people with great difficulties in this area. They can confront their perfectionism and other irrational beliefs that often underlie conditional self-regard and the unrelenting effort to prove they are always right and correct.[4]

2. **Mutual influence and openness.** Decision makers try to influence each other, but avoid dominating. Controversy requires people to persuade, inform, and convince to make the discussion stimulating and involving. People have the conviction and willingness to argue their posi-

tions forcefully and to persuade, but they avoid dominating and coercion. They say, "I want you to consider this seriously," and, "You will probably find this convincing," not, "You must accept this point," and, "You have no choice but to agree." There is give-and-take, not dominance or passivity.

Taking Stock

1. **Examine the solution.** Discussing opposing views openly does not inevitably result in superior decisions. A solution that appears satisfactory one week may seem ineffectual the next. Be prepared to recycle through positive conflict to dig into a problem further and create alternative solutions.

2. **Assess the process.** Decision makers do not expect to discuss opposing views well without practice. They reflect on how they used conflict productively. They make realistic plans to strengthen their capabilities.

3. **Celebrate.** Using conflict to make decisions is challenging, but the rewards are considerable. People recognize their abilities and efforts, the quality of the solution, and confidence in their relationships. They jointly celebrate their success.

Guides for Action

- Elaborate positions and ideas.

- List facts, information, and theories.

- Ask for clarification.

- Clarify opposing ideas.

- Challenge opposing ideas and positions.

- Reaffirm your confidence in those who differ.

- Identify strengths in opposing arguments.

- Search for new information.

- Integrate various information and reasoning.

- Create a solution responsive to several points of view.

Pitfalls to Avoid

- Assuming your position is superior.

- Trying to prove your ideas are "right" and must be accepted.

- Interpreting opposition to your ideas as a personal attack.

- Refusing to admit weaknesses in your position.

- Pretending to listen.

Conflict Model of Organizational Decision Making

Organizations must respond to changes in technology, international competition, and consumer preferences to update present approaches. Most researchers are highly skeptical that decision makers are able to consider these new situations fully and create appropriate solutions. The traditional, rational model of decision making is today considered an unrealistic picture of how people in organizations actually solve problems. The rational approach proposes that people comprehensively identify their goals clearly and search for all available alternatives. They then predict the consequences of implementing each of these alternatives. Finally, they evaluate the alternatives and choose the one that best promotes their original goals. The decision makers are expected to know where they want to go, recognize and be able to consider all possible approaches, and then dispassionately select the best.

Researchers have pointed out that this rational approach is based on the false assumption that people can process and consider a great deal of information.[5] Indeed, there are many studies documenting these limitations. In identifying the problem, analyzing it, developing alternatives, considering consequences, and selecting the choice, individuals have been found to be closed to new and opposing information, to fail to evaluate information adequately, and to have an unwarranted confidence in their conclusions. For example, they often dismiss information that opposes their point of view, simplify the relevant consequences to be considered, and use early trends to draw conclusions prematurely. Despite the tendency to commit these errors in judgment, individuals have been found to be quite confident that they are right.[6]

Researchers have argued that a more realistic view is that decision makers in fact seek solutions that are "good enough" rather than the best. They do not have the abilities and resources to explore issues fully or to create specific solutions. Rather, they use old solutions or slight modifications to try to cope with emerging problems.

A second major criticism of the rational approach is that decision making in organizations is not so much an intellectual activity as a social and political one.[7] It is based not on reason, but on conflict. People and groups, though in the same organization, have differing interests. They form coalitions and sometimes collude in order to further their own objectives. Intellectual disagreement is not so much a different view of what is right, but a way to get what one wants. Yet this way of making decisions can be functional because the most critical groups are in a better position to use political processes and make compromises. Important groups get what they need to continue to contribute to the organizations. This political model is considered a more realistic view of power in organizations.

The idea of positive conflict challenges the assumption that conflict interferes with comprehensive decision making.[8] The positive-conflict model of organizational decision making accepts that individuals have limited perspectives and ability to consider information and alternatives. People and groups are expected to have different points of view and interests. *By engaging in constructive controversy, individuals help each other cope with the biases of closed-mindedness, simplistic thinking, inadequate evaluation of information, and unwarranted commitment to their position.* They use this conflict to understand opposing positions, develop alternatives, and integrate apparently disparate positions into creative, high-quality solutions.[9]

The conflict-positive approach presents neither an optimistic nor a pessimistic view of decision making. It does indicate that people have a choice about whether they are to solve problems effectively or not. They can combine their insights and manage their biases; through a productive discussion of their opposing views, individuals can together explore issues, develop new alternatives, and commit themselves to new solutions. But managers and employees do not have to collaborate in this manner. They can—and they often do—suppress their opposing views or discuss them in a competitive, win-lose way, and thus make safe choices and costly mistakes.

Concluding Comments

Harmony, traditionally much lauded, undermines decision making. When managers suppress their differences, they can make poor decisions that threaten the credibility and vitality of the company. They remain ignorant of risks and opportunities, and make decisions without thoughtful analysis. They court disaster as well as stagnation.

People working together can open-mindedly explore, combine ideas, and create solutions. To solve problems together, managers must express their opposing views openly. In controversy, managers, confronted with an opposing position, are apt to doubt their own position, ask questions to explore alternatives, take opposing information seriously, develop a more accurate view of the situation, and incorporate opposing positions into their own thinking and decisions. Through conflict, decision makers come to understand opposing positions, develop alternatives, and adopt creative solutions.

But not all conflict of ideas is useful; conflict must be well managed. Controversy, like other kinds of conflict, needs to be discussed cooperatively and skillfully. The decision makers must understand that having opposing views does not mean that they have opposing goals and objectives. The computer team all wanted the best possible design that would best serve Lee, the people who used the computer system, and themselves. They knew that what was important was not that their original position be right and accepted, but that Lee have the best possible decision.

Debates over decisions, though they provoke feelings, are focused on differences in ideas. But a great deal of conflict is grounded in irritations, grievances, and anger, as people frustrate each other in attempting to pursue their own objectives and responsibilities. These conflicts have more of a raw edge as interests and actions clash. People at Lee had to manage these conflicts as well, and the next chapter describes how the chief accountant and Rick negotiated their differences on budgets.

References

1. R. A. Cosier and C. Schwenk, "Agreement and thinking alike: Ingredients for poor decisions," *Academy of Management Executive* 4 (1990): 69–74. D. W. Johnson, R. T. Johnson, K. A. Smith, and D. Tjosvold, "Pro, con, and synthesis." In B. Sheppard, M. Bazerman, and R. Lewicki (Eds.), *Research on Negotiations in Organizations* 2 (Greenwich, CT: JAI Press, 1990), pp. 139–74. D. Tjosvold, *Working Together To Get Things Done: Managing for Organizational Productivity* (Lexington, MA.: D.C. Heath, 1986).

2. F. Murray, "Teaching through social conflict," *Contemporary Educational Psychology* 7 (1982): 257–71.

3. D. Tjosvold, "Participation: A close look at its dynamics," *Journal of Management* 13 (1987): 739–50.

4. A. Ellis, "The impossibility of maintaining consistently good mental health," *American Psychologist* 42 (1987): 364–75.

5. H. A. Simon, *Administrative Behavior* (New York: The Free Press, 1976).

6. C. R. Schwenk, "Cognitive simplification processes in strategic decision-making," *Strategic Management Journal* 5 (1984): 111–28.

7. R. M. Cyert and J. G. March, *A Behavioral Theory of the Firm* (Englewood Cliffs, NJ: Prentice-Hall, 1963). J. Pfeffer, *Power in Organizations* (Boston: Pitman, 1981).

8. D. Tjosvold, "Implications of controversy research for management," *Journal of Management* 11 (1985): 21–37.

9. K. M. Eisenhardt, "Making fast strategic decisions in high-velocity environments," *Academy of Management Journal* 32 (1989): 543–76. K. M. Eisenhardt and L. J. Bourgeois, III, "Politics of strategic decision making in high-velocity environments: Toward a midrange theory," *Academy of Management Journal* 31 (1988): 737–70.

6

Negotiating and Mediating

I know I am among civilized men because they are fighting so savagely.
Voltaire

I hold it to be a proof of great prudence for men to abstain from threats and insulting words toward anyone, for neither... diminishes the strength of the enemy; but the one makes him more cautious, and the other increases his hatred of you and makes him more persevering in his efforts to injure you.
Niccolo Machiavelli

"I think there's definite, but not dramatic, improvement," Steve said, as Dale sat down to talk about the conflict program. "I liked the report on where we should be heading with the computer system. We need more planning and fewer crises. I hear less rumbling between the computer group and users, but there're still problems."

"I think we have made some progress," Dale said. "Michael, the others in the computer group, and people like Rick have all been open and willing to deal with the problems. We are developing a good environment, but there's more work to be done so that people actually discuss and make use of their conflicts. The managing of conflict needs to be institutionalized...part of how people work at Lee."

"I guess we have to take a long-range view of this."

Dale argued that getting other groups involved in the conflict-positive program would reinforce the message of managing conflict and support the computer team. Dale did not want the program to come across as "fixing-up" the computer group. He wanted to get all the groups within the organization oriented to making conflict positive.

Steve knew that conflict was a two-way street and a company-wide issue. From his position, he saw people with different responsibilities slugging it out. He was glad that people took their roles seriously, but the infighting pained him. He knew his reminders to be more gentle were ineffectual; he had uneasily concluded that it was human nature for competent, ambitious people to fight.

Steve asked Dale to talk to Sara Johnstone, the chief accountant. She was, he added, a professional with current ideas, but also with troubles. The production and computer groups agreed that the accountants were "bean counters" who piled on paper work but did not make cement. Sara seemed strong in her position, but he worried that the pressures might be getting to her. Last month she had come into the office, and as they discussed her links with Rick, Michael, and other managers she had become very upset. Steve did not want to lose Sara and have to train another accountant.

Dale met Sara in her office in the administration building, which was set apart from the operations building that housed the production, maintenance, and computer groups. She looked even younger than her 33 years. She was reserved and cautious, but had a quick smile. She turned serious as they got down to business.

She wanted Dale to know that she liked her job and making cement. To her it was much more rewarding to work in a place that made something than to work in a public accounting firm. She took her role as the person in charge of preparing the financial reports for auditing and the managerial reports for the company very seriously. She wanted zero-based budgeting, realistic forecasts, and clarified variances. These were procedures any modern company needed.

Her voice softened as she talked about her problems with other managers. "I've tried to be clear about what I am trying to do, but they don't listen. I have spent so much time explaining the whys and hows of accounting that I can hear myself in my sleep."

"Why do you think they are so closed to your ideas?" Dale asked.

After some thought, she said, "I think it must be that they just don't have any training in accounting." She couldn't think of more concrete reasons.

Dale reaffirmed that his mandate was to improve conflict management at Lee. Steve and Tom wanted people to deal with their conflicts more directly and openly. He proposed that she meet with the other managers for a frank exchange of positions.

"I don't want to be ganged up on," she responded.

Dale assured her that the purpose of the meeting would not be for others to blame her, but for a sharing of views, and that he would be there to mediate.

"Perhaps I can talk to one of them rather than the whole group. Rick I can usually talk to."

Dale agreed and then went over the negotiation ground rules that he wanted her and Rick to follow. (See Negotiation Procedures later in this chapter.)

Rick was in a good mood as they began the meeting. The plant was running smoothly and was making cement. He had some self-doubts about hammering things out with a college graduate, but he liked the give and take of conflict and dealing with an ongoing irritant. He also liked talking to women. Sara was more nervous and uptight.

Dale explained that their purpose was to discuss how the accounting and production departments worked together, and to identify problems and conflicts. The discussion was not to end conflicts, but to begin dealing with them. His role was to facilitate communication and help them manage their conflicts; he was not the judge and jury of who was right and who was wrong. He summarized the basic steps of negotiation and placed them on an overhead projector. Both of them had been asked to be prepared to present their views.

"Our accounting procedures are in disgraceful shape," Sara began. "What we do is very much contrary to my values and beliefs. You should see the auditors when they look at the shambles we call our budgets and signing authorities. It is just not the way to budget."

Rick enjoyed the excitement of the discussion, but wanted to make sure that his views did not take a back seat. "You say our budgets don't look good. I'm not into being pretty. Making cement is not a pretty business. Come on down and we will show you how dirty we get when we are making cement. We can't be worried about how nice it all looks on paper."

"I am not talking about appearances," Sara said self-righteously. "I am talking about planning wisely, keeping within budgets, and justifying any discrepancies. I don't care what business you're in, you have to do these things."

"It does matter what business we're in. We're in the cement business, and we have a billion-dollar investment out there that we have got to keep working. Remember, no one does anything here, no one gets paid a cent if we don't make cement. You're insisting on paper work, justifying this and that, making our vendors develop long contracts, and so on, when we are knocking ourselves out getting the mill back."

Dale watched as they argued and counterargued. In his younger days he would have jumped in earlier and "put them back on course," but he had learned that it was easy for an outsider to think the conflict discussion should be "efficient." The people involved are usually deeply engaged in elaborating their point of view and confronting one another. Time goes by much faster for them than for observers.

Dale did not want the discussion to stall at this stage, and when they began to repeat arguments, he said, "Now I hope you both remember that you should be listening, because we now move into the next phase: putting yourself in the other's shoes." Dale pointed to the procedures on the overhead.

"You take all the fun out of this," Rick teased.

Sara and Rick had been taking notes and both used them to reflect back what they had heard. Again Dale was careful not to rush them and to give them time to demonstrate what they had learned and for the other to clarify and correct.

"Now that you're both satisfied that you understand each other's basic arguments, let's try to define the problem specifically. We can also identify the costs of the conflict to both people."

"I'm too stubborn," Sara said with a laugh. But the candor surprised them all.

"Stubbornness is a company trait," Rick said.

"I'd like to get a bit more specific," Dale joined in the fun.

Rick and Sara cited lack of communication, listening, and time as underlying the problem, but Dale wanted them to be more focused.

They decided that the problem was that the aspects of accounting—budgeting, signing authority, and explaining variances—were not presented and considered in the context of making cement. They were seen as extraneous and burdensome rather than as a tool. Sara would tell them this is the way to budget and the production people would nod, but saw no compelling reason to do things "her" way.

Dale asked them to brainstorm what the costs of this approach to accounting were to them. Rick said he was more aware that the present budgeting procedures cost him, Sara, and the whole plant. The overruns made his department look disorganized to corporate officers. One reason the corporate office pressured Steve and Tom, who in turn pressured him to keep the kiln moving, was because they expected cost overruns from the plant. They had little confidence in Rick's projections. This discussion helped him understand the trapped feeling he had of working hard (and spending money) to please the higher-ups who kept on wanting more.

They also more clearly appreciated how the chaotic procedures made Sara look bad. Sara realized more fully the great pressure on Rick to keep the kiln moving 24 hours a day, seven days a week.

These costs made it clear that they should invest in finding ways to develop budgeting procedures that were, and were seen as, useful. It was clear to them that they and others at Lee would benefit from a resolution of the conflict. They needed to make cement, but they had to do it in an efficient way and document that to the corporate officers.

Their understanding of each other and the importance of working on the issues directly and together was real progress, but they had to continue to discuss and involve others. They had found their common ground, but still had to create solutions. Additional brainstorming and decision-making sessions were needed to develop the training and procedures in budgeting necessary for accounting to support production fully.

Mediation

Dale mediated the conflict between Rick and Sara. His goal was to improve the openness and skill of the communication and problem solving so that they could work out the problem effectively for mutual benefit. He judged himself on how well he created the conditions for a productive discussion.

He did not dictate the procedures nor arbitrate a solution, but he was nonetheless active and influential. He outlined useful steps, kept track and encouraged progress, was prepared to intervene if one side was intransigent or abusive, and was ready to derail any major side-tracks. He did not try to take power away from Rick and Sara, but to empower them to resolve the conflict and arrive at their own solution.

The Manager as Mediator

Managers at Lee, like those of every organization, get involved in other people's conflicts. Subordinates will complain about each other and vent their frustrations with other departments. Colleagues will ask them for advice. They will be in meetings where people fight and cajole. Managers must be skilled in dealing with others' conflicts.

The key to dealing with other people's conflicts, as with managing one's own, is being able to choose the appropriate approach and carry it out successfully.[1] Conflicts are too varied for one approach always to be effective. Managers are inquisitors, judges, motivators, advisors, investigators, restructurers, and problem solvers. When employees are in conflict, they listen, give advice, avoid getting involved, tell them to solve their own problems, or impose a settlement. Unfortunately, many managers are trapped into predetermined ways of responding to employee conflicts.

A traditionally popular approach is to tell the warring employees to knock it off. The manager wants no more bickering, complaining, and gossiping, and threatens to punish, perhaps fire, the guilty. A progressive version of this approach is to understand the conflict, develop a solution, and then impose it upon employees. Many managers assume that their role is to end all disputes: they must seek out all the facts, determine who is right and who is wrong, and make and enforce a decision.

Imposing a solution and warning employees that they better stop bickering works in some situations. Managers are satisfied that they have exerted leadership through decisive action and have ended the conflict efficiently. Yet the shortcomings of this approach are not well appreciated. The manager, despite exhaustive work, may be unable to understand the situation fully or create a useful solution. Imposing the solution is even more difficult. Employees often believe that the solution is biased against them and that the manager has treated them unfairly. They remain angry toward each other, but are now angry with the boss as well.

Mediation should be used much more often than it is.[2] Managers mediate by helping employees manage their conflicts. They encourage employees to use good conflict procedures and skills. They must discuss their ideas and feelings openly, emphasize their common goals, demonstrate interest and respect for each other, and seek resolutions that are mutually beneficial. *The mediating manager is referee and resource person rather than judge and arbitrator.*

In addition to avoiding the pitfalls of imposing settlements, skillful mediation results in the benefits of positive conflict. Frustrations are expressed and reduced, problems are understood, the best ideas from several persons are put together to create solutions, and the partners to the conflict accept and implement the solution and feel better about themselves and their work relationship. The manager is satisfied that he has helped his employees both solve their own problems and become more skillful. *The manager who mediates will be less burdened with future conflicts, for the employees will be able to handle them independently.* But mediation requires managers and employees to be skillful and patient.

Alternative Dispute Resolution In and Out of Organizations

Conflict spills out across organizations as disputes arise over contracts, rights, and obligations. Judges, legal reformers, and social scientists are spearheading a movement to use private-resolution processes as an alternative to the formal justice system. They argue that the huge financial and emotional costs of our "litigious" society and the overloading of the judicial system make using alternatives imperative.[3]

Alternative dispute resolution typically entails having the antagonists voluntarily and in confidence seek the assistance of an independent, impartial, and skilled third party. A range of procedures can be employed. In *confidential listening,* the neutral third party discovers each side's "bottom line," and if there is overlap, informs the conflicting parties that they can reach an agreement that is at least minimally satisfactory to each. In *conciliation,* the third party engages in shuttle diplomacy, trying to open up communication and identify common ground. *Mediation* is similar, though the mediator serves as a facilitator as the protagonists meet face to face to try to reach an agreement.

A *mini-trial* has also been used successfully. Senior officials from each company hear the best-case arguments submitted by the companies' employees who are in dispute. Then, with the third party, the senior officials try to hammer out an agreement. In *neutral-case evaluation,* an expert in the area of dispute serves as a third party who, after listening to counsel from both sides, gives a nonbinding opinion. In *med-arb,* the mediator first conducts mediation, and if this fails renders a binding arbitral award. *Arbitration* is established in the law, and its particular form depends upon the jurisdiction. Typically, an expert serves as a third party, listens to both sides, who are often represented by counsel, calls witnesses, retains experts, and then renders a legally binding decision.

Alternative dispute resolution procedures are being used within organizations as well as between them.[4] Managers act as conciliators as well as mediators and informal arbitrators. Organizations have ombudsmen to serve as neutral third parties. However, whether used in or between organizations, these procedures, possibly with the exception of arbitration, require positive conflict to be effective. The third party and the antagonists need to learn and use the skills and values of positive conflict.

Negotiation Procedures

Negotiating conflicts productively requires persistence, skill, and ingenuity. Sara and Rick used the following guidelines to help them negotiate their conflict.

Value Diversity

1. **Develop a Positive-Conflict Attitude.** Conflict needs to be accepted as inevitable and potentially constructive. People have relationships characterized by mutual concern and respect that allow them to discuss issues directly and compassionately. They work to improve everyone's ability to deal with conflict. When everyone is strong psychologically, conflict can be well managed.

2. **Confront the Problem.** People openly confront their difficulties and differences, and focus on the problem. As they express their own views, they invite others to do the same. They let each other know how they experience the conflict. They communicate their ideas, feelings, and hopes to clarify the issues and release tension. They include the facts, goals, interests, and information that lie behind their positions. They avoid surprises and do not catch people off guard, but select a situation when both

have the energy, time, and openness to discuss the problem.

3. **Put Yourself in the Other's Shoes.** Conflict is an opportunity to understand another's feelings, views, and thinking. People ask about and try to understand each other's perspective so they can appreciate the problem fully, understand all sides, and be in a better position to develop solutions that work for all. They stop defending their own views long enough to listen carefully to others, and demonstrate their understanding by repeating the other's position and arguments. People who believe others are trying to, and do, understand them, are open to listening to others and resolving the conflict.

Seek Mutual Benefit

1. **Jointly define the problem.** Conflicts defined specifically to everyone's satisfaction are more easily resolved than general principles and grand ideas. People fight over issues, not personalities. They identify specific behaviors (how they develop the budget) rather than personalities (the accountants are bossy and arrogant). They stick to the issue and main problem without bringing up tangential issues that diffuse and confuse. They avoid taking the discussion too personally, feeling indignant, or trying to save face.

2. **Find motivation to resolve the problem.** It takes two to have a conflict and two to untangle. People who realize that their own interests as well as others' are harmed by the conflict are motivated to pay attention and act on the conflict. People can discuss the costs and benefits for continuing versus resolving the conflict. When conflicts escalate, people tend to underestimate the costs of fighting and the benefits of stopping. When everyone realizes the costs and the benefits, discussion is apt to be fruitful.

3. **Establish cooperative goals.** Parties to a conflict easily forget their common ground. In a positive-conflict situation, no one person is blamed because responsibility is shared, and it is recognized that everyone has contributed to the conflict. The parties focus on working together to manage the conflict, not finding fault. The

problem is defined as a mutual problem for everyone to solve, not a struggle to see who will win. They communicate that they intend to work for mutual benefit. The emphasis is on win-win solutions in which everyone gains.

Empower

1. **Show respect and acceptance.** Reaffirmation of the value and competence of others contributes to productive conflict. Throughout the discussion, people show respect and acceptance of each other. They avoid challenges and insults that question another's competence and morality. Disagreements are not taken as challenges to one's face that must be defended.

2. **Follow the golden rule of conflict.** The golden rule of conflict is simple but often misunderstood and ignored. It is: *use approaches that you want others to use.* If you want people to listen to you, then listen to them. If you want them to take your perspective, then take theirs. If you want others to compromise, then you compromise. The golden rule is one way to influence others, even those perceived to be unyielding and closed-minded.

3. **Use appropriate strategies.** Negotiation is more likely to be successful if people, though they are firm in pursuing their own interests, are flexible in their methods and approaches. They may use *cost cutting,* in which one person gets what he or she wants while cutting the other person's costs in conceding. Or they may try *logrolling,* in which each person agrees to the other person's demands in areas of primary importance to that person— no one gets all that he or she wants but they both get what they most want. *Bridging* is sometimes possible. Here a totally new option is developed that satisfies the interests of all.

4. **Reach an agreement.** Conflict is an opportunity to get new information and to understand issues more completely. Putting oneself in someone else's shoes allows more creative solutions to emerge. Many prolonged, intense conflicts in organizations must be solved through repeated discussions.

Take Stock

1. **Reaffirm the Agreement.** People show good faith by implementing the agreement and checking to make sure it is working as expected. They reflect on the discussion and recognize the areas that could be improved.

2. **Celebrate.** People recognize the courage and skill it took to work out the conflict productively and how their ability to manage conflict will help them greatly in the future. They appreciate that people worked and took risks to resolve the conflict, and they celebrate their success.

Guides for Action

Value Diversity

• Set norms that conflict will occur and can be useful.

• Confront problems and communicate feelings openly.

• Try to understand the views and feelings of others.

Seek Mutual Benefit

• Define the problem together.

• Understand the costs of fighting against the conflict and the benefits of resolving it.

• Focus on working together to manage the conflict for mutual benefit.

Empower

• Show respect and acceptance of others as people.

• Use approaches that you want others to use.

• Use strategies of cost cutting, logrolling, and bridging.

- Reach an agreement.

Take Stock

- Reaffirm the agreement by implementing it.

- Evaluate the solution and look for ways to improve it.

- Celebrate successfully negotiating the conflict.

Pitfalls to Avoid

- "We don't have time."

- Assuming others' goals oppose yours

- Using one strategy for all circumstances

- "It's your fault"

- "Me…Me…Me"

- "Us vs. Them"

- "Either-Or"

- "Got ya!"

Barriers to Positive Conflict in Negotiation

Valuing diversity, sharing aspirations, empowering, and taking stock contribute to constructive negotiation. Tough obstacles remain for negotiators, however.

Avoiding Conflict

Employees have many reasons for avoiding confronting their frustrations and differences. Time constraints, group norms against fighting, a commitment to a public image of harmony and maturity, and an exaggerated sense of one's vulnerability and the other's strength can all get in the way. Sara felt vulnerable in the face of the powerful production group.

Physical separation is a growing reason for delays in negotiating. In today's organizations, people in different locales, even in different countries, may be asked to work together. It can seem extremely difficult to deal with conflicts over the telephone or computer network.

Fighting to Win

People in conflict often assume that their major goals and objectives are opposing. They assume that the conflict is competitive, and they hesitate to deal openly with it. The computer and production groups assumed that each was trying to make the other look bad and that they were uninterested in making cement or in strengthening their relationship.

In most conflicts, people have a choice about how they want to frame and think about how their goals are related. Sara can assume that her procedures have to be followed or not, that she will either win or lose. Alternatively, she can think of the conflict in terms of broadening the accounting perspective at Lee so that it is as useful as possible for helping Rick and others make cement efficiently and effectively. Though she may not get all she would like, she can get a great deal and maintain a relationship for future success.

Rigidity

Many people are rigid in their approaches to dealing with conflict. They feel they must attack, soft-pedal, or be highly rational in every conflict. Negotiation requires flexibility and attempts to find new ways to hammer out new ways of working.

Negotiation requires both giving and taking. People have to communicate their frustrations and needs, argue for their interests, demand satisfaction. But at the same time, they have to be flexible, willing to compromise, and able to see how they can pursue the other's interests as well. Successful negotiators are both firm in their demands and fair in responding to others.[5]

Keeping Conflict "Undiscussable"

With low levels of conflict, people feel there is not much reason to examine and strengthen their approaches. However, as conflict escalates and explodes into angry outbursts, they become frightened and overwhelmed, and informal discussions over coffee and stepping into each other's office disappear. Formal scheduled meetings and workshops are often necessary to open up lines of communication.

Concluding Comments

The conflict between production and accounting was based on opposing actions and interests. Sara's work to fulfill her role and be seen and rewarded as a competent accountant who contributed to the company interfered with Rick's efforts to manage crises and spend whatever money was necessary to get the mill working again. As they pursued these respective responsibilities, they clashed and quarrelled.

They used negotiation not to relinquish their interests but to find ways to accommodate and reconcile them. They exchanged, defended, and modified proposals to reach an agreement that promoted their needs. They used offers, counteroffers, and persuasive arguments. They prepared their positions, presented them, and defended them from criticism. They challenged the positions of one another, but also came to see how they could work together to make each other better off. Eventually they worked out an agreement.

The previous chapter examined the conflict of ideas, also called controversy. Controversy involves intellectual disagreement in which people have arrived at different conclusions about what is right, just, and effective. They resolve this conflict through elaboration of their arguments and reasoning. People in controversy may have no opposing interests or goals: they all want the best decision for the group but differ as to what should be adopted.

Most conflicts are blends of controversy and conflict of interests. Negotiation often resembles controversy, especially the integrative bargaining used by Rick and Sara. They engaged in argumentation, elaboration, and incorporation of different points of view characteristic of constructive controversy. They identified underlying essential problems and began to generate possible solutions, but kept decisions tentative until they had developed a package of solutions that satisfied their initial concerns but gave neither of them their original demands.

Conflict can provoke feelings of annoyance and anger as well as an intellectually stimulating debate of opposing conclusions and negotiation of different interests. An important challenge is dealing with strong feelings so that the conflict is positive. The next chapter explores how anger can be channeled in ways that are productive for the organization and its people.

References

1. D. M. Kolb, "Who are organizational third parties and what do they do." In R. J. Lewicki, B. H. Sheppard, and M. H. Bazerman (Eds.), *Research on Negotiation in Organizations,* Vol. 1 (Greenwich, CT: JAI Press, 1986), pp. 207–78. B. H. Sheppard, "Third party conflict intervention: A procedural framework." In B. M. Staw and L. L. Cummings (Eds.), *Research in Organizational Behavior,* Vol 6 (Greenwich, CT: JAI Press, 1984), pp. 141–90. R. Karambayya and J. M Brett, "Managers handling disputes: Third-party roles and perceptions of fairness," *Academy of Management Journal* 32 (1989): 687–704.

2. R. E. Walton, *Managing Conflict: Interpersonal Dialogue and Third-Party Roles* (Reading, MA: Addison-Wesley, 1987).

3. B. Thompson, *Alternative Dispute Resolution: A Canadian Perspective.* Canadian Bar Foundation, Ottawa, 1989.

4. W. L. Ury, J. M. Brett, and S. Goldberg, *Getting Disputes Resolved: Designing Systems to Cut the Costs of Conflict* (San Francisco: Jossey-Bass, 1988).

5. D. G. Pruitt, *Negotiation* (New York: Academic Press, 1981).

7

Making Anger Productive

In headaches and in worry
Vaguely life leaks away.
        W. H. Auden

I was angry with my friend:
I told my wrath, my wrath did end.
I was angry with my foe:
I told it not, my wrath did grow.
        William Blake

"I had trouble sleeping for several nights after we talked with Rick," Sara told Dale. "I just couldn't relax."

Dale was surprised; he didn't like surprises for much the same reason that Rick didn't like them. He might be unprepared and vulnerable. "I'm sorry to hear that...I didn't expect that...I hope you're okay."

"I think I've recovered."

"What happened? You didn't seem that upset after the meeting."

"I wasn't...I felt good. But afterwards I just couldn't stop thinking about it all. My mind went around and around."

With some probing by Dale, Sara talked about how she would suddenly feel a sense of power and release, then feel depressed and worn out. She would think warmly of Rick, Michael, and others at Lee and then feel upset.

She was worried about her psychological health. For some time she had a run-down feeling with little energy. She was shocked when told she was developing a peptic ulcer. Her physician thought she may be demoralized and recommended assertiveness training.

"I've been thinking—not sleeping at night gave me a lot of time to think—that my troubles have to do with conflict," she continued. "As I was brought up, the one clear lesson I was told over and over again was that getting angry and into conflict were wrong. When I went to college, my accounting professors hammered away at being a professional and mature. Lee is definitely a man's world, and people there are supposed to be tough and unemotional: 'We make cement.' Now you come along and tell us to let it all hang out."

"You're thinking that the talk with Rick opened up your strong feelings that you had tucked away."

"I think so. I've always seen myself as a person who is very serious about her career, but also very socially minded and responsible. I like people; I don't want Rick to be mad at me."

"I can see why you might think that being a professional, working with your colleagues, and wanting them to like you are inconsistent with getting angry. But they aren't."

"You're confusing me."

Dale explained that feeling angry is very much a part of wanting to do a good job and have good work relationships. If you don't care, you don't get angry. People get angry at people who are close and important to them. Why would one get angry at someone who means little?

"But you don't see a lot of yelling and screaming around here, at least not in the administrative office."

Dale argued that there are a great many ways that people express their anger. They bite their lips and tongue, play sports, run marathons, use sarcasm and put-downs, tease, and are stubborn and testy. And there are lots of ways people try to avoid anger. Some people take the offensive and scowl and snarl to scare people away. Others take the defensive and are highly submissive and subservient.

"I think I belong to the stubborn camp. Perhaps that's why I can be so bull-headed. Like Rick was saying the other day, I start out gentle, but quickly get set and determined to get my way. And he becomes just as determined. I surprise myself by how stubborn and upset I get. But it does irk me that production always seems to get its way and we accountants are just seen as nuisances. It's not right."

"We should talk in more depth about these matters some day. But I think a common reason why people get very angry is because they keep telling themselves that others should not get in their way, should do what is good for them, should not criticize them...that others have no rights. Often people feel a sense of powerlessness to do something about it. Then we become self-righteous, and then the stubbornness, revenge, and even rage come out in force."

"Interesting, but difficult to get a handle on. I'm going to have to think about this."

"Accepting, valuing, and using anger are much different than we usually have been brought up to believe and aren't part of the way we've been trained to think and act as professionals. But we need to find ways to express anger directly. I hope that managing conflicts more openly at Lee will provide legitimate, useful ways to channel and use anger."

"So you *do* want us to let it all hang out," Sara teased.

"Only after the 'Revolution,' " Dale said, with a laugh. "Lee, you, and me and the rest of the world aren't ready for that. I know many bosses who do not expect, will not tolerate, being the target of anger. Many people will take it in small doses, but do not want to be 'dumped on.' People in organizations need alternative ways to deal with anger, including how to channel it indirectly. In addition to expressing anger directly, exercise, relaxation training, even forgiving and forgetting all are important in managing anger on and off the job."

Misuse of Anger

I never let the sun set on a disagreement with anybody who means a lot to me.
Thomas Watson, Sr., founder, IBM

Many of us in business, especially if we are very sure of our ideas, have hot tempers. My father knew he had to keep the damage from his own temper to a minimum. A practical salesman, he knew his legacy would depend on his ability to turn a vision into reality.
Thomas Watson, Jr., chairman emeritus, IBM

Sara gets angry and annoyed at Rick when he appears to dismiss her budget procedures. Rick is irritated that Sara is so stubborn and apparently unwilling to bend to the realities of crisis management. There are many other emotions in conflict. Rick laughs and enjoys the give and take of negotiating with Sara. Sheldon feels challenged to defend his plans for a new computer design. The computer team is proud that it used an intellectual discussion to develop plans they believe in.

Anger poses the most challenges and hazards of the emotions in conflict. Conflict itself is a test. If handled well, the conflict strengthens and reaffirms relationships, but if handled poorly, conflict can rip them apart. Anger is in turn a test of conflict. If managed, anger contributes to the productive power of conflict. Unmanaged anger intensifies conflict and feeds more anger and disruption.

Sadly, *anger is the most misunderstood, the most repressed, and the most mismanaged of all emotions.* Anger is commonly thought to signify immaturity and a lack of personal control and mastery. A manager's angry outburst fuels suspicion and mistrust. It challenges his image as an outgoing, approachable person or as a firm-handed, respected disciplinarian. Angry employees are fired; highly angry people are locked up in prisons and institutions.

Despite economic progress and psychological sophistication, we may have more trouble handling anger than our ancestors did. Social scientists refer to this as an "angry age." Murder and abuse statistics, "crimes of passion," headlines of terrorists and violence, and stories of stabbings over minor traffic infractions all suggest uncontrolled anger and rage.

Traditional organizational values are highly anger-negative. Organizations have been thought of as "machines" in which people are supposed to be "businesslike" and devoid of feelings. Progressive companies are expected to have shared values and a common mission and to serve their customers industriously. Employees should have bosses and colleagues who care about them, listen to their feelings, and provide a sense of support and caring that enhances self-esteem. The current emphasis on "up-beat, positive" values often leaves little place for anger.

In spite of intentions, anger will not be shoved aside or driven away. It affects individual well-being and organizational functioning, whether people want it to or not. Sara thought of herself as a mature professional and caring person who, therefore, does not get angry. Her idealism left her anger unmanaged, and her repressed anger contributed to her feeling demoralized and powerless and to her rigidity in dealing with her colleagues. As a result, she felt even more frustrated and powerless, and Lee did not have costs under control or credible budgets.

The key to managing conflicts productively is to develop a strong sense of mutual dependence and pursuit of common interests.

Unfortunately, how anger is handled often interferes with people feeling that their conflict is cooperative. Conflict is often mismanaged in organizations because anger has been allowed to degenerate it into a win-lose, "I'm-right,-you're-wrong," competitive struggle.

What Leads to Feeling Angry?

Conflict occurs when people believe that others are interfering, obstructing, or in other ways getting in their way. Anger is based in part on the experience of obstruction, but anger is more than frustration.

We get angry when we hold another responsible for our frustration and believe that that person had no legitimate reason for interfering with our efforts and could have avoided doing so. Anger is based on the perception of an *avoidable, unjustified frustration.* The target of anger is thought to have done the misdeed deliberately with no compensating rationale. People who obstruct us with sufficient reason or without intention or knowledge may annoy, but not anger us. We are angry when a colleague leaves us extra work because he or she wants to lie on the beach, but not when he or she has to attend a sick child. Anger appears to be particularly strong when others are thought to be illegitimately obstructing our ability to improve our self-esteem and social status.[1]

Anger derives from how people think about and experience conflict. Rick and other production people at Lee were angry with the computer group because they held that group responsible for what they believed was an unreliable computer system that caused them much grief. It galled them that the computer group was paid well to help them, but often didn't. They felt that if the computer group would take serving them more seriously the system would make them less anxious and their work less grinding.

Production did not have to be angry. With another perspective, they could have reacted much differently to their troubles with the system. If they had thought the computer group was highly motivated and on their side, they may have assumed that the computer glitches were unavoidable and therefore would not have blamed and been angry with the computer group. Their conflicts would have been seen as problems to be ironed out, not battles to be fought.

Anger and Positive Conflict

Contrary to popular beliefs, anger is not an antisocial force. People who were asked to keep detailed daily diaries of their feelings of anger and irritation were found to get angry with other people, seldom with inanimate objects.[2] Most often they got angry with loved ones and people they liked, and sometimes with acquaintances. The least likely target of anger was people they didn't like.

Anger brings life to conflict and conflict to life. It is common to argue and hope that if people could be rational and sensible— meaning without anger—then conflict would be well managed. However, anger is central to important conflicts. It is unmanaged and suppressed anger that makes people wary of confronting conflict, doubtful about the value of differences, disruptive of cooperative goals, and feeling powerless.

Open, skillful anger contributes significantly to positive conflict. As shown in the list below, it promotes confrontation of differences, emphasizes cooperative dependence, reaffirms people's power, and focuses attention on frustrations.

Value Diversity

Awareness. Anger is a signal that helps people scan and know what is happening. Discovering they are angry leads them to search for frustrating and unproductive events and conflicts.

Energy. Anger mobilizes and increases the vigor of actions. People can use this energy to deal with problems and achieve their goals.

Seek Mutual Benefit

Reaffirms dependence. People usually get angry with people who are important to them. Anger is fundamentally a sign of dependence and of valuing other people.

Strengthens collaboration. Skillful anger communicates that the person wants to work out difficulties and problems in order to improve working relationships to get things done.

Empower

Defense against anxiety. Anger transforms internal anxiety to external conflict. Anger overcomes fears and inhibitions to help people take action, defend and protect themselves, and feel more confident and powerful.

Sense of righteousness. Anger gives people a feeling of virtue and being right despite the opposition of others. They are willing to speak out and challenge people to manage the conflict.

Take Stock

Focus and motivation. Anger disrupts ongoing behavior by making people agitated and interfering with normal information processing. They want to correct the perceived injustice and counter the aggression. Expressing anger gets the attention of others and motivates them to deal with the conflict.

Negative feedback. Angry people often feel released to express suppressed frustration and negative feedback. This communication identifies problems that can be dealt with and solved and thus strengthens the relationship.

Conflict without anger can be shallow and unproductive. People who do not experience their anger may be unaware of frustrations, blame themselves for being demoralized, and feel powerless. When people do not express anger, others are uncertain if the problems are important and worthy of their attention. Nor do they understand the grievances or feel compelled to act.

Toward an Anger-Positive Organization

Anger is often an unwelcomed challenge and threat. Traditional ways of organizing and managing leave people cautious about expressing their anger directly. However, more anger-positive values, roles, attitudes, and sensibilities can help employees use anger to deal with conflict productively for mutual benefit.

Values

Traditional prejudices and organizational values imply that "negative" emotions like anger have no legitimate place in the workplace. Expressing anger is seen as counterproductive and harmful—a sign of "lack of cooperation." Anger quickly orients employees to think that they must protect themselves and possibly counterattack the aggression. *Organizations need values that support the skilled expression of anger as legitimate and potentially useful.*

Dale wanted the people at Lee to *value the role of anger.* He would describe an ideal work relationship not as one devoid of troubles and frustrations, but as one in which people could share their feelings and hammer out solutions that worked for them. He encouraged and provided settings for people to talk about their anger and other feelings and solve their problems.

Roles

Many managers assume that their role requires them to be in charge and in control. With this control orientation, they quickly assume that any anger directed at them is an attack on their competence as managers. They feel they must suppress the conflict to reassert their authority.

Dale wanted Michael and other managers to adopt more *realistic role expectations* of working and managing. Michael should not look at himself as the expert who had all the answers, but as a resource person who would work out new computer programs with users. Michael should not think of Sheldon as a troublemaker who made him look bad, but as a committed worker willing to help Michael identify problems to improve the computer team and assist Michael's leadership. *Managers need to enlist anger, not suppress it.*

Attitudes

Despite talk of shared vision and common mission, there is a great deal of mistrust in many companies. Employees do not have a firm belief that co-workers have their interests at heart. They suspect that others are self-interested, unconcerned, and willing to take advantage of them if it is expedient to do so. People engage in gossip, office politics, and power struggles. Under these conditions, anger is used and will be thought to be another strategy designed to get one's way at others' expense.

However, *a sense that "we are in this together" and that "we can rely on each other" helps employees respond positively to anger.* Reawakening the understanding that the people at Lee had the common goal to make cement effectively was the major thrust of Dale's work. People had thought that they were committed to making cement, but doubted others' motivation. The computer group thought production workers just wanted to get through the day; production thought the computer group wanted to stay dry, clean, and rested in their offices. Dale encouraged talking, having lunch together, spending time together, and celebrating joint successes so that people would feel they could *trust others to work for common objectives.*

Sensibilities

Individuals have their own assumptions that make them experience anger as a challenge and an attack on their "face" of competence. They counter such affronts with tough, intransigent actions that escalate conflict.[3] Some people quickly assume that anger directed at them is an attack and their best defense is to counterattack. They feel anger is never justified and always meant to harm. The irony is that while they believe anger is very negative, they get angry every time someone gets angry with them! *Employees with the more realistic, useful view that they cannot be right and perfect under all situations and will at times make errors and irritate others cope more successfully with anger and conflict.*

Dale counseled Sara that *feeling angry was part of being a serious professional and wanting good relationships.* She did not have to assume that feeling angry challenged her view of herself, or that others' anger toward her was unacceptable. A more realistic view of anger would leave her more relaxed and open-minded.

Skills to Manage Anger

An organization that accepts and values anger is an important first step. But anger is often suppressed because people do not have confidence that they can deal with it openly. Managing anger is challenging and requires considerable competence. Dale led workshops for the people at Lee to refine and develop their skills to monitor and change their anger, express their anger directly and indirectly, and deal with angry colleagues.

Choices

Anger is often experienced as an unexpected feeling that comes over one and takes control. Intense anger can strike quickly and subside just as quickly. People report that they are unable to stop themselves from getting angry and losing control. Yet *we control anger, anger does not control us.* Unfortunately, many people are unaware of how they choose to be angry.

Other people do not make us angry. Our conclusions that their actions were frustrating, intentional, and illegitimate do. By changing our thinking we can change our emotions. If Michael takes Rick's outburst as a gratuitous attempt to coerce him and make him look bad, he gets angry. If he sees that Rick is venting his legitimate frustration because he's had to delay his vacation to get the kiln back moving, he feels compassionate.

Although getting angry may seem like a quick step or no step at all, it is a complex process of attributing responsibility and drawing inferences and conclusions. People do not have to put themselves into "automatic" and get angry without being aware. They can operate in "manual" and decide when they will get angry. *They do not let others push their button.* They realize that they can change their feelings by changing their thinking.

Coping with Anger and an Intolerable Boss

Perhaps the most trying situation an employee can find himself or herself in is to have a boss who is not just unaware or unfriendly, but is mean, nasty, and competitive. Getting such a boss is bad luck, but at least it is shared. Three-fourths of the highly successful in three *Fortune 100* companies reported that they had had at least one intolerable boss during their careers.[4]

Very few of them openly confronted this intolerable boss, and even fewer actually changed their boss or got the organization to demote the boss. But most were able to cope. They tried to minimize their feelings of anger and their desire for revenge. They accepted the boss as the boss. They gave up feelings that the boss should not act as he or she did, and did not concentrate on perceived unfairnesses and injustices. They downplayed their own frustrations, and even thought about the situation as one they could learn from. They tried to understand the pathologies and perspective of the boss. They knew the kind of boss they did not want to be; they learned that they wanted to be patient and respectful.

The executives changed their thinking, so they weren't so angry. Then they were able to plan ways to work around the boss. They avoided situations that triggered the boss's anger and used his or her periods of good mood to advantage. They talked to friends, exercised, and used other ways to vent their feelings.

Research indicates that we have choices about how we deal with and express our anger. Indeed, people find it easier to control what they do than control how they think about angry situations.[5] People verbally lash out and punish, but they also talk to the person without hostility, talk to others to get their perspective, ventilate, gossip to get back, and take their anger out on others. People are by no means programmed to deal with anger in one way; they have many options.

Expressing Anger

Although not every angry feeling should be expressed to the person held accountable, this approach is direct and has the most potential to initiate a productive conflict. There are several rules to keep in mind when expressing anger.

- **Check assumptions.** No matter how convinced employees are that someone has deliberately interfered and tried to harm them, they may be mistaken. People can ask questions and probe. It may be that the other person had no intention and was unaware that others were frustrated. The incident may just dissolve into a misunderstanding and annoyance.

- **Be specific.** People find being the target of anger stressful and anxiety provoking. They fear insults and rejection. The more specific the angry person can be, the less threatening and less of an attack on self-esteem the anger is. Knowing what angered the other can give the target of the anger concrete ways to make amends.

- **Be consistent.** Verbal and nonverbal messages should both express anger. Smiling and verbally expressing anger confuses the issue.

- **Take responsibility for anger.** Persons expressing anger should let the target know that they are angry and the reasoning and steps they took that made them feel unjustly frustrated.

- **Avoid provoking anger.** Expressing anger through unfair, insinuating remarks ("I can't believe someone can be as stupid as you!") can make the target of the anger angry too. Such situations can quickly deteriorate.

- **Watch for impulsivity.** Anger agitates and people say things they regret later.

- **Be wary of self-righteousness.** People can feel powerful, superior, and right; angry people can play, "Now I got'ya and you will pay." But anger should be used to get to the heart of the matter and solve problems, not for flouting moral superiority.

- **Be sensitive.** People typically underestimate the impact their anger has on others. Targets of anger often feel defensive, anxious, and worried. It is not usually necessary to repeat one's anger to get people's attention.

- **Make the expression cathartic.** Anger generates energy. Telling people releases that energy rather than trying to submerge it. Anger is a feeling to get over with, not to hang on to.

- **Express positive feelings.** Angry people depend upon and usually like people they are angry with. People expect help from people who have proved trustworthy, and are angry when it is not forthcoming.

- **Move to constructive conflict management.** Feeling affronted, personally attacked, and self-righteous should not side-track you from solving the underlying problems. Use the anger to create positive conflict.

- **Celebrate joint success.** Anger tests people's skills and their relationships. Be sure to celebrate the mutual achievement of expressing and responding to anger successfully.[6]

Ventilating

Direct expression of anger toward the person held accountable is not always possible or desirable. It may not be wise or practical to confront an intolerable boss, a new customer, preoccupied colleagues, and stressed employees. Even when direct expression is possible, it is often useful to express it indirectly first so that it is not strong and overpowering.

- **Exercising.** Vigorous and active activities such as running, swimming, racket sports, and fast walking are useful.

Shouting, screaming, crying, throwing things, and punching pillows release energy.

- **Talking to others.** People spend a great deal of time confiding, complaining, and gossiping. When others listen, such talk helps reduce the power of anger. When they encourage revenge, talking with others intensifies anger.

Changing Unrealistic Assumptions

Anger is natural and inevitable, but some people find themselves frequently angry. They may be abusive and may alienate friends, as well as continually upset their own mood. Often these people have unrealistic assumptions that lead them to think about situations in ways that make them very angry. Some common assumptions include the following:

- As I am a good person, everyone should like and respect me.
- Every person who gets angry at me has acted unjustly and unfairly.
- Every criticism is designed to make me look foolish and weak, and my self and social respect demand that I counterattack.
- God gave me the right to an uninterrupted lunch hour (or chair, traffic lane, or whatever), and anyone who infringes on this right is wrong and no longer a worthy person.[7]

Employees should know their own assumptions, realize how they affect their interpretations of situations, identify assumptions that lead to overly angry feelings, dispose of these assumptions, and replace them with more reasonable ones.

Conflict and anger situations can help in this learning. As people realize they have jumped to wrong conclusions, they become aware of the faulty assumptions. Then they develop more useful assumptions, and argue with themselves until they adopt them. People have learned misleading assumptions; they can replace them by learning more useful ones.

Constructive assumptions include:

- Although I am a good person, I will do things that will upset and frustrate others.
- People who get angry with me often value me and our relationship and want to deal with problems and make our relationship stronger.

Figure 7.1
Managing Anger

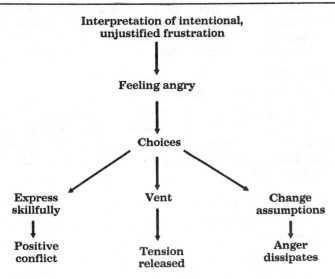

- Criticism and negative feedback can help me become more self-aware and stimulate the motivation to improve my competence and upgrade my skills.

- It would be nice if I was left in peace for my lunch hour (no one used my chair, no one cut me off in traffic), but these are nuisances that I can easily live with.

Using Anger Skills at Lee

Often people must combine the skills of expressing anger directly, venting their feelings, and modifying their thinking and changing assumptions. Computer-group members were learning to cope with specific provocations by the production department. For many years, production people—very agitated about problems they blamed on the computer and the computer group—would burst up to the second floor and let out their anger. They did not always follow the guides for expressing anger outlined in the above section!

These outbursts got the attention of the computer group, but they also provoked them to become defensive and to counterattack. They would often stay cool on the outside, but burn on the inside, and try to show (rationally, they said) how the person was all wet and that it was not a computer problem. In effect, they argued that the production people did not know what they were talking about. This implication was not lost on the production people, who countered with more anger and disgust. These incidents had soured the climate and work relationships.

The computer group had the unrealistic expectation that the production people should change and be diplomatic. The production people had the unrealistic expectation that the computer group should fix every problem in the plant. The stalemate dragged on for years.

The computer group worked with Dale to develop a more constructive approach to these provocations. There were concrete steps the computer group could take before, during, and after the provocation to help them cope and make these outbursts less wearing and damaging, and they could even take steps to develop better work relationships.

Before the provocation, they developed more realistic expectations. They reminded themselves of the pressure the production people worked under and the frustrations they encountered. The production people had different but not necessarily inferior ways to express themselves. It was not realistic to expect them to communicate in the same ways that computer professionals do. Perhaps it would be nice if they were very polite and calm, but that expectation was not realistic and it would do little good to get upset because they were upset.

The computer group wanted to feel that they could be in charge and in control even if the production people seemed out of control. They were not going to let their buttons be pushed and get all upset when they knew it would not do any good.

During the provocation, they experienced the outburst and worked to cope with it. They would not take attacks on the computer system or the group personally, and reminded themselves that emotional statements should not be taken literally; the production person was letting off steam, and as soon as the person had released his or her frustration, they could begin to problem solve. There was no need to doubt themselves, even if the production person did. They knew they wanted to take the long view, not try to counterattack because that would continue the negative conflict in which everyone loses.

They wanted to show the production people that despite verbal attacks, they still wanted to solve the underlying problem. They wanted to avoid discussions of who was to blame and who was responsible, and to find a solution that worked in the short term and in the long term as well. They did not want to use the outburst as another example of why the computer group was more knowledgeable, civilized, and superior to the production department.

After the outburst, they celebrated their strength and success in keeping cool and in charge of themselves and the situation. They shared their experiences with others in the computer group and gave each other suggestions about how they could be better prepared to respond to future provocations.

Concluding Comments

Managing anger is one of the most pressing and difficult challenges for people in organizations. Suppressed anger can lead to debilitating stress, physical illness, and emotional turmoil, while angry outbursts are taken as signs of immaturity and lack of personal control. When confronted by angry persons, people sometimes feel threatened and counter with their own self-righteousness. But *anger, when skillfully managed, can initiate positive conflict.*

Attitudes toward anger are changing. Instead of being seen as a negative emotion that leads to disruption, we are learning that feeling angry can provide the energy to confront differences and strengthen relationships. Often when cooperative goals are recognized and the motivations are understood, anger is channeled into a search for productive solutions to problems.

The challenge for Sara and others at Lee was to understand that they could change the way they responded to anger. Sara was beginning to recognize that her anger stemmed from her deep desire to be a competent professional respected and valued by her colleagues. She went behind these constructive motives, however, to adopt a mischievous, destructive assumption that she had to be right and correct in all that she did. Feeling appreciated and developing more realistic expectations would help her feel less angry and demoralized. She could also learn to adopt other ways to express her anger than blaming herself and others. Indeed, her anger could be channeled to encourage positive conflict and resolve problems.

Examining conflict and anger is a way to understand the personal beliefs and interpersonal skills of Lee employees. But the culture and structure of Lee influenced how Sara dealt with anger and negotiated with Rick about accounting procedures and how Michael and the computer team discussed their differences regarding the overall design of the computer system. Steve was recognizing that work to develop the culture and structure of Lee would promote positive conflict. The next section explores how companies can strive to become united, team organizations that serve their employees as well as their customers.

References

1. J. R. Averill, *Anger and Aggression: An Essay on Emotion* (New York: Springer-Verlag, 1982).
2. Ibid.
3. D. Tjosvold, "Social face in conflict: A critique," *International Journal of Group Tensions* 13 (1983): 49–64.
4. M. M. Lombardo and M. W. McCall, Jr., *Coping with an Intolerable Boss* (Greensboro, NC: Center for Creative Leadership, 1984).
5. J. R. Averill, *Anger and Aggression.*
6. D. W. Johnson and D. Tjosvold, "Managing stress and anger in conflict." In D. Tjosvold and D. W. Johnson (Eds.), *Productive Conflict Management: Perspectives for Organizations* (Minneapolis: Team Media, 1989), pp. 193–215.
7. A. Ellis, "The impossibility of maintaining consistently good mental health," *American Psychologist* 42 (1987): 364–75.

Part IV

A Positive-Conflict Culture and Structure

Since Fredrick Taylor, influential management theories have assumed that conflict was negative and that managers should structure organizations to minimize friction. Individuals were assigned specific roles and tasks and had established channels of communication. Managers had the authority and power to coordinate work and resolve any dispute.

The knowledge that conflict, when well managed, is productive and contributes very significantly to collaboration has far-reaching implications for structuring and managing organizations. Traditional values and procedures must be examined and new ones adopted that prepare managers and employees to use conflict. Rather than avoiding conflict and pretending it is not there until it escalates out of control, employees use opposing ideas to make decisions, negotiate their differences, and deal with their anger to strengthen their relationships and get things done.

Chapter 8 describes how positive conflict helps create a feeling of company unity and common direction that in turn sets the stage for valuing differences and conflict and seeking mutual benefit in dealing with them. Positive conflict and organizational unity are mutually reinforcing.

Chapter 9 argues that teams are concrete ways to structure positive conflict in organizations. Well-managed teams create the structure and rewards for positive conflict. Teams show that diverse perspectives solve organizational problems, assign people a common task with shared rewards that build cooperative goals, provide the forum and expectation for ongoing communication and collaboration, and highlight the need for taking stock and continual development.

To inspire the best from their employees, companies have to demonstrate that they are just and ethical. While there are some generally agreed-upon absolute rules, justice is mostly a matter of balancing differing and at times opposing views and interests. How can a forest products company reconcile its goal to produce wood and paper at a reasonable cost, yet minimize its negative impact on the environment? How can a company treat a loyal, but careless employee fairly, yet maintain the safety of the plant? Chapter 10 argues that positive conflict is needed so that people come to understand and appreciate how the company is trying to reconcile different values and competing claims. Positive conflict draws attention to ethical issues and helps deal with them.

8

Forging a United Direction

If a man does not know to which port he is sailing, no wind is favorable.
Seneca

A shared vision, the common goal to serve customers, and other cooperative aspirations give companies, groups, and individuals direction and meaning. They challenge us to train and sharpen our abilities, and inspire us to apply our energies and work together to get things done. Work without a common direction frustrates us because we do not know where we are going and whether others will help.

Positive conflict, as it celebrates diversity and encourages opposing views, might seem at first glance to be antithetical to a common mission and unified direction. But positive conflict builds organizational unity; unity lays the groundwork for positive conflict.

A common direction supports positive conflict for it emphasizes cooperative interests and shared aspirations. Employees have a strong sense that, though they disagree, they are very much on the same side and will seek "win-win" solutions. Vision and goals also provide benchmarks for resolving conflict. Disputes and opposing views can be resolved on the basis of which decisions best move employees along their common direction.

Positive conflict helps create a meaningful vision to which all employees are committed. Visions must be developed and become common through dialogue and discussion, not by decree. People find a common direction through reconciling their individual hopes.

Conflict to Create a Shared Vision

A vision expresses the essence of company goals and philosophy in a way that captures the hearts and minds of employees. People know the aspirations and expectations for their organization, team, and themselves, and are committed to achieving them.

But to create such a vision, executives, managers, and employees' management must engage in ongoing debates about the company's mission and strategy. Researchers have recognized that conflict in the top management team is critical to hammer out a unifying strategy from the various perspectives within the company.[1] But top management must also be open to the ideas and frustrations of managers and employees to develop a practical strategy. Employees themselves must understand and be convinced and committed if the vision is to be lived and implemented. They contribute to the ongoing development of the vision; at least, they can ask questions and get answers so that they understand the vision and its implications for their group and themselves. This involvement and questioning inevitably involve conflict.

Disciplined Creativity

Envisioning is a creative process. Leaders and employees must look beyond the everyday distractions of work to ponder the future of what things might be like. They challenge, experiment, and innovate. Various opinions and positions must be encouraged to identify what is broken, challenge the status quo, and break out of the mundane. Articulating frustrations specifies problems and barriers that are blocking progress and need changing.

Envisioning is also a disciplined process. A vision is supposed to unite people so that they feel on the same team. For that to happen, *the opposing ideas and interests must not only be expressed but reconciled.* Through conflict management, people reach an agreement on their fundamental direction. Although it is seldom necessary for everyone to agree on every issue, a vision requires an overall consensus.

Discipline is also required so that groups make their own visions and objectives complement those of the company. A department's vision takes on meaning as it relates to and supports the work of other groups. A CEO has more leeway in influencing company direction, but even at that level there are constraints. The vision must build upon the present capabilities and orientations of the people and groups within the company. Abrupt change in vision is very costly and risky, and under most conditions de-motivates rather than inspires. Envisioning is not unrestrained creativity, but requires that conflicts be managed and discipline achieved.

Disrupting Win-Lose and Avoid

Efforts to form a vision that degenerate into win-lose fights rip apart the group and company. But avoiding conflict also undercuts the value of developing a vision. Smoothing over differences and opposing views results in inferior decisions. People remain emotionally uninvolved and feel removed from the vision and the company. If they believe they cannot speak out and must follow the company line, they are apt to feel especially frustrated and conclude they should not care so much about the company and its direction.

A family that owned and managed a chain of hardware retail stores became highly committed to a vision statement that they hammered out over three days. However, when middle management asked questions and commented on the vision, the family members quickly felt attacked and the sessions turned to win-lose fights. The family managers withdrew from discussing the vision and tried to put the experiment behind them. However, tensions were never worked through and the attempt at a vision developed wounds and divisions that lasted for years.

Poorly managed conflicts make even beginning to create a unifying vision problematic. The hostility between the computer and production groups at Lee Cement, for example, made it difficult for them to see that they had a common vision or work together to develop one. Their suspicions, stereotypes, and anger could have easily exploded as they talked about a shared vision. However, as they managed their conflicts they were coming to believe that they were both committed to making high-quality cement.

Positive Conflict for a Credible Vision

Through listening to opposing ideas and frustrations, leaders demonstrate concretely that they want everyone on board and committed to the vision. Indeed, the process of developing the vision shows the way the vision will be achieved; that is, by means of dealing honestly with differences and trying to reconcile various perspectives so that the people can be a united, powerful force.

The method of developing a vision suggests how to achieve the vision. *The open discussion and coming together that are neces-*

sary to create an engaging vision are also needed to accomplish the vision. Creating a common direction requires positive conflict; positive conflict is needed for people to work together to strive for the vision. Without such consistency, the vision is apt to seem like high-sounding platitudes and create the impression that the vision is not being "lived": managers are talking the talk, but not walking the walk, and this breeds cynicism.

A vision then should include positive conflict as a way to achieve the vision. Making positive conflict a part of the vision contributes to managing conflict. Employees recognize that others also want to deal with conflicts openly to promote company aspirations. A common direction and positive conflict reinforce each other and develop a constructive cycle of organizational development.

Uniting to Serve Customers

You have to be sincere when dealing with people, and that includes the public and your employees.
Isadore Sharp, Chairman, Four Season Hotels

Some companies make the mistake of telling employees what to do to get close to customers. Good external service requires good internal service.
John Cunningham, President TMI (North America)

Customers are first, employees second, shareholders third, and the community fourth.
Credo, H.B. Fuller Company

Serving customers gives managers and employees a tangible, unifying direction and is central to the vision of nearly all organizations. An organization—whether it be a political party, a consumer company, or an educational institution—that loses touch with its constituents is in danger. Customers provide the resources and support needed to sustain an organization. Companies have been forcefully reminded that they must listen, understand, and respond to their customers.[2] Less recognized is the fact that *conflict is critical to serving customers.*

The popular saying "the customer is always right" implies that businesses do not manage their conflicts with customers so much as avoid them and give in. But selling involves developing relationships with customers and managing conflict. Conflict also affects the delivery of goods and services. The unmanaged conflict between production and computer groups interfered with Lee's capacity to deliver high-quality cement to customers. Positive conflict was being put to work to help serve Lee's customers.

Research on Conflict with Customers

Members of the sales force are the customers' most tangible contact with the company. If customers feel they have been served in a cold, insensitive manner, they are likely to feel put off and may even consider going to other companies. A surly bank teller who makes the correct deposit but leaves the customer feeling irritated and unfairly treated has harmed the bank. How salespeople treat the customer cannot be separated from the company's products.

Effective sales representatives must then establish cooperative, positive-conflict relationships with customers. They need to be oriented to the customer, not just to making a sale.[3] They must take the time to know their customers, work to solve their problems, and serve their interests. They must be expert communicators who know their products and their customers, and must develop personal bonds with them that lead to reliable, repeat business.

A recent study indicates that positive conflict contributes substantially to the sales relationship. Sales representatives of a large airline and their large customers, namely, travel agents and personnel in charge of corporate travel, were interviewed.[4] It was very important to the travel and businesspeople that the sales representative deal directly with their problems and concerns. When the representatives failed to listen or dealt with issues in a rigid way, customers felt frustrated and lost confidence that they would be effectively served. The statistical analysis revealed that positive conflict contributed greatly to a strong customer relationship.

Companies are recognizing that responding to customers' complaints is not an after-sale nuisance, but contributes to their success. They can learn more about the quality of their products, how the company does and does not meet customers' needs, and strengthen their relationship with customers. Positive conflict is needed to keep in touch with customers.

Research on Coordination and Customers

Coordination and conflict management within a company affect how customers are treated.[5] Dynamics within the firm affect the salespeople's mood and treatment of customers. If the manager of the bank grumbles and complains all day to the bank tellers and makes them feel unsupported and unfairly treated, it will be difficult for them to be warm and accepting of customers. They can easily let out their own frustrations as they deal with customers. Moreover, a supervisor who does not manage conflicts openly with employees has not shown them how they can deal skillfully with customer complaints.

Coordination also affects the quality and delivery of products. For example, marketing high technology requires considerable coordinated effort. The sales representatives, the engineers and technicians who modify machinery to fit client needs, the training group that teaches the skills to use the technology, and the support group that installs and repairs equipment were found to need to resolve their conflicts so that customers received the technology that met their needs.[6]

Conflict was also found to be very useful for employees in a large engineering firm.[7] The business-development, finance, project-management, pulp-and-paper, steam-and-power, civil-and-structural, and mechanical-engineering groups needed to express different ideas and iron out difficulties to present a unified proposal to clients. Once a proposal was accepted, they had a large number of conflicts that they had to manage constructively to complete the projects. Similarly, people from eight groups within a customer service division (250 employees) of a utility had to identify problems and integrate different views to deal effectively with customer complaints.

Positive conflict is needed to promote the coordination among individuals and groups necessary to deliver high-quality products to customers. Companies need to respond to complaints and deal with conflicts from customers. In addition, positive conflict helps employees hammer out how they can make the company more customer-oriented.

Vision and Serving Customers at Lee

Based on his past experience and his position as general manager, Steve worried about the future market for Lee's cement. The foray into the California market was paying off now, but Steve was concerned that Lee may be the "first out" if the market turned down. Others at Lee felt much less urgency; they had, perhaps quite understandably, a more short-term perspective, and that demanded an emphasis on making more and more cement. They nodded at Steve's urging to pay more attention to the customers. They dismissed it as the influence of Steve's latest book.

Steve did not want to avoid this issue, nor did he want to pound his fist, demanding that something be done or heads would roll. That approach would have created much activity, but mostly of the "appease-the-boss-until-he-gets-off-his-high-horse" kind. He recognized that he would have to involve the people and groups at Lee so that they understood the importance of serving their customers well.

Steve and Dale thought that the biweekly management meetings at which Tom, Rick, Michael, Loren, Greg, and other managers met to discuss common concerns would be a suitable forum for discussion. Steve argued his position that the market, though now very strong, could change quickly. He believed that they needed to develop strong customer loyalty by serving the customers well to retain business in a downturn, and he wanted the group to explore how they could do that.

The discussion began haltingly. Then Rick lit the fires by charging that not everyone was on the same side and all were not equally committed to making cement. Sometimes production felt like it was the only group interested. Others protested and challenged Rick. Sara argued that she wanted to make cement, but in a planned, cost-efficient manner. Skip Jordon from the laboratory charged that at times production didn't seem interested in quality and didn't take his group's analyses seriously.

The discussion highlighted the confusion and the fact that there were different understandings of the actual vision for Lee. Groups focused on different aspects of the business. Somehow, quantity, quality, timeliness, and cost-effectiveness had to be integrated. Steve argued that Lee had to continue to experiment with high-performance cement to be prepared for the future.

The meeting left the managers energized but with no clear way of proceeding. They were more aware of issues and problems, but were unsure what they could do. Over the following weeks, the managers agreed on a plan of action. They would ask for volunteers from a cross-section of the plant to begin developing a common vision for Lee. The team's charge was to use the managers' previous discussions and their own ideas to bring forward a tentative vision for the company and suggest procedures for people to discuss the vision. It was not enough to develop a written statement, people had to understand and buy into the vision. This vision should identify their customers, how Lee should serve them, and how the departments could work together to succeed.

The process of developing a shared vision should help the company cope with the problem that groups at Lee do not feel equally important. Production is widely regarded as the most essential; its people feel free to complain about other departments, but are closed to hearing complaints in return. Assuming they are the most important, their attitude focuses on "what other departments should do for us." What's needed is a sense that all departments are valuable and that by working together they make high-quality cement in reliable volumes at reasonable costs.

The shared vision should frame company objectives in ways that show that all the departments must work together to be successful. How can departments be committed to their own departmental tasks, yet identify strongly with the company and see that to be successful as departments, the whole company must succeed?

Positive conflict focused Lee on the need for a shared vision; conflict would be part of the ongoing process to create it. The task-force members would continue to debate what the vision should be and how they can get people involved and behind the vision. The task force would also have to deal with conflict with the management group as it presents, defends, and extends its recommendations. Finally, positive conflict will help describe how the vision of quality cement efficiently produced and delivered on time can be realized. The production, computer, accounting, and other groups must collaborate effectively and manage conflict to produce quality cement in a timely manner to serve Lee's customers and strengthen the job security and pride of Lee employees.

Concluding Comments

Positive conflict is needed to create and achieve a common direction. It is not enough in an organization that the CEO or the department manager has a vision. Indeed, a vision to which only the leaders are committed divides managers and employees, rather than bringing them together. Dialogue and conflict are needed so that everyone understands and feels a part of the common direction. To remain alive, the vision needs to be continually updated and made fresh and relevant.

Means and ends are often confused. It is easy to assume that because the goal is to find a common direction the way to do that is through agreement. But the *consensus has to be hammered out and unity forged.* Opposing ideas, frustrations, and different interests cannot be papered over, but must be openly expressed and dealt with so that a common direction is forged.

References

1. R. A. Cosier and C. Schwenk, "Agreement and thinking alike: Ingredients for poor decisions," *Academy of Management Executive* 4 (1990): 69–74. K. M. Eisenhardt, "Making fast strategic decisions in high-velocity environments," *Academy of Management Journal* 32 (1989): 543–76. K. M. Eisenhardt and L. J. Bourgeois, III, "Politics of strategic decision making in high-velocity environments: Toward a midrange theory," *Academy of Management Journal* 31 (1988): 737–70. D. C. Hambrick, "Putting top managers back in the strategy picture," *Strategic Management Journal* 10 (1989): 5–15. D. C. Hambrick, "The top management team: Key to strategy success," *California Management Review,* Fall (1987): 89–108.

2. T. J. Peters and R. H. Waterman, *In Search of Excellence* (New York: Harper & Row, 1982).

3. F. R. Dwyer, P. H. Schurr, and S. Oh, "Developing buyer-seller relationships," *Journal of Marketing* 51 (1987): 11–27 D. R. McDermott and C. N. Schweitzer, "Product vs. customer focus industrial selling," *Industrial Marketing Management* 9 (1980): 151–57.

4. D. Tjosvold and C. Wong, *A Study of Interdependence in the Sales Relationship.* Manuscript, Simon Fraser University, 1989.

5. D. E. Bowen and B. Schneider, "Services marketing and management: Implications for organizational behavior." In B. Staw, *Research in Organization Behavior* 10 (Greenwich, CT: JAI Press, 1988), pp. 43–80.

6. D. Tjosvold and C. Wong, *Collaboration to Market High Technology: A study of Goal Interdependence.* Manuscript, Simon Fraser University, 1988.

7. D. Tjosvold, "Cooperative and competitive interdependence: Collaboration between departments to serve customers," *Group & Organization Studies* 13 (1988): 274–89.

9

Teams for Positive Conflict and Synergy

[After managers and workers] come to see that when they stop pulling against one another, and instead both turn and push shoulder to shoulder in the same direction, the size of the surplus created by their joint efforts is truly astounding. . . .This. . .is the beginning of the great mental revolution which constitutes the first step toward scientific management.
    Fredrick W. Taylor

We have a great team spirit. Our people want to be the Marines. They want to be the finest. We hire eagles and teach them to fly in formation.
    Wayne Calloway, CEO, PepsiCo, Inc.

People can get satisfaction from a group effort. . . .This is good for business, because in an industrial organization it's group effort that counts. There's really no room for stars.... You need talented people, but they can't do it alone. They have to have help.
    John F. Donnelly, President, Donnelly Corporation

A common vision contributes to positive conflict. Though they disagree, employees feel on the same side and try to resolve their differences to promote their common direction. Yet a vision cannot stand alone: assignments, roles, resources, and rewards must reinforce collaboration and positive conflict. This chapter argues that *well-structured work groups, task forces, and project teams provide forums and incentives to manage conflict productively.*

The stereotype that harmony and teamwork go together causes great damage. Employees assume that a manager who espouses teamwork is telling them to agree and not speak out, and the manager gets frustrated because the employees seem uninvolved. Many of the prejudices against groups—that they sink to the lowest common denominator, suppress individuality, and encourage sheeplike passivity and group think—are rooted in the assumption that they avoid conflict.

But positive conflict is a critical reason that teamwork has so much value. *Teams have great potential in large part because they allow for diverse contributions and perspectives and forge them into an integrated approach.* However, to realize their potential through positive conflict, teams have to be well structured and managed.

Potentials of Teams in Organizations

To create companies that can respond nimbly to a turbulent marketplace and create competitive advantages, managers are experimenting with various types of organizational teams.[1] Quality circles, task forces, project teams, semiautonomous work teams, new product rugby, labor-management cooperation, parallel structures, the Scanlon plan, and gainsharing programs, though they have different philosophies, language, and focus, all involve the explicit use of teams to accomplish important organizational tasks. Teams are becoming the basic building blocks of organizations.

Largely unrecognized is the fact that positive conflict is a major reason for the potential of teams in organizations. *Teams are practical ways to foster positive conflict that results in integrated effort.* Professionals and employees can combine their specialized knowledge to develop unified solutions that work from various perspectives. Teams implement participation and gain employee involvement. Although it is impractical to have large departments gather to debate issues, their representatives can create a consensus.

Teamwork and Positive Conflict

Groups are not magical answers to all organizational ills, nor do they automatically make a company a winner in the marketplace. Teams have great potential, but there are pitfalls and problems that threaten them.[2] Forming teams is not by itself an effective strategy. *Positive conflict provides an elegant way to understand and manage groups so that they are productive.* Conflicts test groups. If they manage conflicts well, then they realize their potential. If they manage them poorly, they degenerate into squabbling anarchy or suppressive group think.

Teams need to be well structured so that employees can conflict productively; promoting positive conflict contributes to successful teams. Well-managed groups highlight employee diversity and the ways in which that can help accomplish goals. They have concrete common tasks and rewards for shared aspirations and cooperative goals. Teams provide opportunities and the mandate to communicate and discuss differences so that employees feel more empowered. Teams must be nurtured and developed; it is vital to take stock and learn from conflicts.

Value Diversity

Effective teams recognize that their diversity helps them accomplish their tasks and increases the fun of working together. A heterogeneous team composed of people who differ in background, expertise, opinions, outlook, and organizational position underscores diversity. Norms that stipulate open communication encourage team members to express their opinions, doubts, uncertainties, and hunches. The right to dissent and free speech reduces fears of retribution for speaking out. Teams structure conflict. Managers actively encourage various viewpoints and indicate that they are willing to change their own position. Successful teams consult various sources. Articles, books, customers, and experts can provide experiences and ideas that can help the group decide which course of action is superior.

Seek Mutual Benefit

Forming teams is a concrete way of developing cooperative goals. Assignments, common rewards, complementary roles, the need to share resources, and sense of common identity promote shared aspirations, which are needed for effective teamwork and positive conflict.[3]

Managers assign their groups a task and ask for one product. The team as a whole is to make a set of recommendations, develop and produce a new product, or solve a problem. Group learning is a particularly important common task. All members are expected to improve their skills in managing, selling, or operating machinery. Team members understand that they will receive rewards depending upon team progress. If the team is successful, then they will receive tangible and intangible benefits. Either everyone is rewarded or no one is rewarded. At 3M, for example, members of new product teams enjoy bonuses and recognition as the product meets established benchmarks in sales. Unproductive groups should be held responsible together. Failure is not blamed on one person, but the team as a whole is held accountable.

Work flow strengthens cooperative goals. Team members recognize that the work of one member depends on the work of others.[4] Complementary and interconnected roles also show how team members must work together. Team members clarify their roles so that it is clear that successful role enactment requires coordinated effort.

The need to exchange and use limited resources highlights cooperative dependence and the need to manage conflict. When each one has only a portion of the information, abilities, and resources necessary to accomplish the task, employees recognize that they all must contribute; alone they cannot succeed. A common identity and trust make team members feel united and prepared to deal with conflict. They feel part of a concerned, accepting group and develop loyalty to it.

Empower

Valuing diversity and unity of cooperative goals prepare team members for making conflict positive. In effective teams, people are confident of their abilities. They know each other's accomplishments, experiences, and credentials, and in other ways realistically disclose their personal strengths. Training programs to improve their communication, conflict, and other group skills are undertaken as needed. Individual team members are held accountable: each one indicates publicly that he or she accepts assigned duties and reports on his or her activities to the group.[5] Failure to fulfill obligations is dealt with by the group.

Teams structure regular opportunities to work together and manage conflict. Formal meetings, having offices close together, electronic mail, and information systems help team members exchange information and keep each other posted. Members have the conviction and willingness to argue their positions forcefully and to persuade, but they avoid dominating and coercion. They strive for consensus through full participation. It is clear that they need a resolution that works from the various perspectives represented in the team.[6]

Take Stock

Reflection contributes critically to team productivity and positive conflict.[7] Teams inevitably have relationship conflicts: people doubt that they really do want to manage conflict openly, are on the same side, and are able to work together effectively. Teams provide opportunities to discuss feelings and deal with issues to strengthen relationships.

The positive-conflict model reminds teams that they need to use frustrations and differences to know each other better and develop more effective ways of working and should continually examine their valuing diversity, shared goals, and sense of confidence and empowering. Team members interview each other, ask for feedback, conduct surveys, and listen to observations to understand their internal workings better. Team members speak their minds about how the team is functioning. They use good feedback skills of describing perceptions and feelings and avoid labeling and evaluation that get in the way of understanding their group's dynamics and managing conflict. The team openly discusses opposing positions about how it should operate and combines ideas into creative, workable solutions for how the team should work together to get things done.

Linking Across Teams and Departments

Teamwork is needed across departments, divisions, and groups as well as within them. Strengthening the departments and linking them together are critical to helping a company become conflict-positive. Cohesion within the departments should not be based on the view that other groups are the enemy.

Synergy between departments is most difficult to achieve. Departments typically do not have specific common tasks or immediate shared rewards to reinforce cooperative goals. Although their salaries, jobs, and prestige all depend eventually upon their common effort, this connection often seems distant. Making the amount of money in employee paychecks, bonuses, or other tangible consequences clearly linked to common success can be unifying.

People in different departments usually do not feel empowered to work together and manage their conflicts. They have few opportunities and settings to discuss issues directly. At Lee, much of the interaction depended upon chance meetings in the lunch room. But this was not the place for serious problem solving and conflict managing. Although having meetings is not enough, a clear mandate and structured opportunities foster positive conflict and collaboration.

Company Teams

Task forces, management teams, budget meetings, liaison teams, project teams, and special-events committees link departments and groups together. Through these interdepartmental teams, representatives of different units bring various perspectives together to achieve common goals. They recognize and appreciate their diversity, emphasize their shared aspirations, feel empowered to work together and manage conflict, and reflect and overcome barriers to forming a united, powerful company.

A critical advantage of company teams is that they give people from different parts of the organization a specific, common task. Most company-wide goals are so general and diffuse that over time that tend to lose their meaning. Company teams are given a specific assignment—to recommend how to make the company more customer-oriented, or to suggest a useful gainsharing program. Members realize that top management believes these tasks are priorities with high visibility within the organization. With this clear direction, employees understand that they have a common, important objective and that, if their group is successful, they will be recognized and rewarded.

It is impractical to have large divisions meet to make decisions, but company teams are practical ways to foster participation. Asking people to join a task force gives them an opportunity to participate and contribute to making important decisions.

Company teams provide a forum to exchange information and discuss ideas. People from different departments have opportunities to know each other, understand their different perspectives and agendas, and develop trust. Cross-departmental task forces encourage direct discussion and exchange.

Though they have great potential, company teams are not automatic solutions. They can alienate, disrupt, and undermine. People can sabotage them and use them to wage war and gain dominance. Company teams must be well managed and, in particular, be able to use conflict positively. Team members should discuss their common assignment so that they feel that their interests and goals are cooperatively linked, and they must work together to be successful. They need the motivation and skills to communicate and make their controversies constructive. Teams must coordinate and manage conflict with people in the organization as they propose and gain support for their recommendations.

American business has been accused of being preoccupied with the short term. Demands to improve the quarterly profit statements and ward off raiders have been seen as intensifying this short-term perspective. But avoiding conflict contributes much to the emphasis on the short term. In many companies, frustrations and doubts linger, but there's no forum where people share their different perspectives. *Company teams with positive conflict can help focus attention on major issues and long-term solutions.*

Conflict and Company Teams

- Diverse perspectives and opinions of people from different departments are brought to bear on important company issues.

- Company teams must be small enough to be manageable and to encourage full participation, but heterogeneous enough to allow for diversity and full representation.

- Company teams provide forums for positive conflict.

- Top management discusses its disagreements and doubts about the recommendations of company teams; it does not simply rubber-stamp or ignore them.

Working Toward Synergy at Lee

Frustrated with the many brush fires and crises, Steve had wanted for some time to develop strong teamwork at Lee. He had tried to not to take sides in disputes and argued the need to work together. But he wanted people to take a stronger, more proactive approach so that Lee would become more of a team and more focused on the long term, rather than getting by day by day.

The management meetings were supposed to improve communication and teamwork at Lee. They did result in more information sharing, but there were few issues—work on the shared vision was an exception—that the group really addressed in any depth.

Steve and Dale discussed the barriers to collaboration. They agreed that developing teamwork between groups seemed more formidable than developing it within groups. However, as they found out with Michael, Sheldon, and the computer group, conflicts within a department are related to conflicts between departments. A strong network within a team helps it reach out to other groups; without this, they may build a fortress for protection and blame others for their frustrations.

Steve and Dale discussed how the departments could strengthen their internal teamwork by seeing themselves as having their own vision that complemented Lee's. Work would be assigned to groups of people, and they would be rewarded to the extent that their groups were successful. The teams would meet regularly to discuss issues and problems. Training programs would help them develop their communication and conflict skills. Team members would be asked to focus on developing themselves as a productive unit over time.

Company project teams, management groups, and task forces were practical ways to strengthen teamwork and positive conflict for Lee as a company. These teams could, like the task force on shared vision, work through the management team. The managers would identify an important issue and ask for a cross-section of interested people to dig into the problem and make recommendations, which the managers and the task force would use to make changes. These task forces would give the issues priority and have a single direction that they could explore in depth. Steve and the managers would not be giving up power, but would use teams to involve more people to help them manage the company more effectively.

Interdepartmental teams could be asked to look at various issues. For example, a task force might be instructed to develop each aspect of positive conflict. For example, how could the departments value and use their diversity? What training and experiences do people need to collaborate successfully? A company team could investigate ways to give everyone at Lee concrete, shared rewards for joint success in pursuing the shared vision; it could visit companies already using gainsharing and profit-sharing plans. Lee would be creating a parallel structure for ongoing organizational strengthening.[8]

Company teams help the management team take a proactive approach to dealing with issues. People from diverse areas tackle significant, long-term problems. They will have to struggle with their opposing perspectives and positions to recommend a plan useful for the company as a whole. After they make their recommendations, they will have to work with the management team and others at Lee to develop a solution people are willing to implement. Company teams explore how to make an organization more synergistic; they also model how different points of views can be integrated.

Support from the Top

Steve and Dale talked more about using task forces to make Lee a team organization that deals with conflict. Dale asked Steve if he would have the support of the head office. He explained that Steve's blessing and support reassured the computer and production groups and others under his authority that they were on the right track in dealing with their conflicts openly, but as the conflict program became more organization-wide, people would feel more committed if they believed that corporate headquarters approved. They would not want to begin, only to get themselves into trouble with the head office, or have it shut them down when it found out.

Steve had buffered the people at Lee from the West Cement head office. When the corporation demanded immediate layoffs, Steve negotiated to reduce staff through attrition. When it demanded no pay raises, he negotiated raises, albeit modest ones. Steve tackled specific issues, but he had avoided the major conflict he had with top management about how Lee should be managed.

The corporate headquarters, as noted earlier, was a tough place to work. The corporate officers saw themselves as very hard-nosed, aggressive businesspeople. They assumed that a basic industry like cement should be run in a no-nonsense way without modern management "frills." They actually had little contemporary experience managing a cement plant. A few had managed, but many years ago. Others had financial, engineering, and legal backgrounds.

Steve grew up working and managing first in the steel and then in the cement business. He knew that the kind of management the corporation favored did not suit him or the people at Lee. He knew that making cement was a people business. He wanted involvement, participation, and commitment. He saw the need for teamwork and managing conflict.

Steve doubted that he could directly address his differences on managing with the head office. Now he was faced with the need to gain their support or at least their neutrality about his work to create a team organization. Dale urged him not to avoid this conflict completely, while assuring him that that did not mean that he would have to initiate a full-blown debate on the best management style. He could present the program in language that the corporate office would find reasonable; he need not emphasize positive conflict and teamwork. He could keep track of absenteeism and other measures to show them that the integration and synergy program was paying off in ways they would appreciate.

Steve wished that he could be more forthright with his corporate bosses and that they would support his efforts enthusiastically, but he knew he would have to persuade and manage them so that over time they could see for themselves the value of the program.

Concluding Comments

Teamwork is much valued, but difficult to achieve, especially between departments. Divisions and groups often lose sight of their common goals and get entangled in argument. Short-term and short-sighted solutions aimed at meeting one department's interests at the expense of others are imposed. Shared purpose is lost, replaced with rivalry, gossip, and blame.

Well-structured teams have common tasks, underline the need for integration, give shared rewards, and provide a forum for discussion, which supports the development of a common vision and positive conflict. They use positive conflict to create new products, use new technology effectively, and develop effective personnel-selection procedures. Indeed, teams are also the means to develop a conflict-positive culture and structure. Company teams recommend how the organization as a whole can develop a shared vision, common rewards, and skills and procedures to promote positive conflict and synergy between departments and groups.

References

1. D. Tjosvold, *Team Organization: An Enduring Competitive Advantage* (New York: Wiley, 1991).

2. Ibid.

3. D. W. Johnson and R. T. Johnson, *Cooperation and Competition: Theory and Research* (Edina, MN: Interaction Book Company, 1989).

4. J. D. Thompson, *Organizations in Action* (New York: McGraw-Hill, 1967). A. H. Van de Ven, A. H. Delbecq, and R. Koening, Jr., "Determinants of coordination modes within organizations," *American Sociological Review* 41 (1976): 322–38.

5. B. Latane, "Responsibility and effort in organizations." In P. S. Goodman (Ed.), *Designing Effective Work Groups* (San Francisco: Jossey Bass, 1986) pp. 277–304.

6. D. Tjosvold, "Participation: A close look at its dynamics," *Journal of Management* 13 (1987) 739–50.

7. W. G. Dyer, *Team Building: Issues and Alternatives* (Reading, MA: Addison-Wesley, 1987).

8. G. R. Bushe and A. B. Shani, *Parallel Learning Structures: Increasing Innovation in Bureaucracies* (Reading, MA: Addison-Wesley, 1991).

10

Reaching for Justice

*Justice is the first virtue of social institutions, as truth is of systems of thought. A theory however elegant and economical must be rejected or revised if untrue; likewise laws and institutions no matter how efficient and well-arranged must be reformed or abolished if they are unjust.**

John Rawls, moral philosopher

"If I hear the words just and fair one more time, I'm going to scream," Tom told Dale as they sat down to talk. "We tell the union we are trying to do as well as we can, we are not out to get them, but that there is just so much money in the pot, and we can't just keep increasing wages and expect to stay in business. We show them our books, we reason with them, but all we get is blank stares and baloney about fairness. Some people just don't want to listen."

"I'm sorry negotiations are not going well," Dale said. "Is there a danger of a strike?"

"We'll settle—we took such a bad strike five years ago that no one wants to do that again—but it's so frustrating. We just can't see eye-to-eye. We think we have been taken advantage of ... they think they've been exploited. The whole atmosphere is polluted."

"I hope you don't mind my using the words, but it sounds like you want fairness and justice too."

"Who doesn't? But they have such a hollow ring to me. It's as if the union uses the words just to badger us and make us feel guilty so that we will give in."

* Reprinted with permission from John Rawls, *A Theory of Justice* (Cambridge: Harvard University Press, 1971).

"It does sound like the words have become part of the fight rather than common ideals to strive for. That needs to be changed, don't you agree?"

"Dale, aren't you being naive? You're always arguing for openness, cooperation, trust, and justice. You're too idealistic."

"You're right that I argue for trying to achieve these values, but I'm not so naive that I believe people are always trustworthy or fair. Justice is not easy to get to." Dale went on to argue that instead of fairness being used against management and the union the two sides dedicate themselves to trying to develop a just organization. Then management and the union would have an important common objective that they could work together to achieve.

"You do remember that we're making cement here, not promoting social welfare," Tom said with both a smile and exasperation.

"So that's why those big trucks keep coming here...," Dale said, trying to add to the humor. "As you know probably better than I, you need a sense of fairness to make cement productively over the long run. Workers grumbling and upset spell a lot of trouble. If they go out on strike, you can't get your billion-dollar investment working or serve your customers. A sense of fairness will make your life and the lives of other managers much more sane."

"But I *want* to be fair."

"Wanting to is not enough. If it were, there would be much more of a sense of fair play in our organizations."

"Wait a minute. You keep telling us to manage our conflicts, now you're telling us to be fair. They don't fit."

"One reason managing conflict is so critical is that it is an important way to develop a just organization. Fairness and justice are not something achieved, but are ideals to strive for continually. And the way to do that is to manage conflicts. Also, a fair organization that people trust makes managing conflict easier."

Positive Conflict to Work Toward Justice

Justice is a powerful word. Injustice provokes anger, even outrage, and demands for change. Injustices not rectified cause rebellion and revolution. The American Revolutionaries were not just frustrated at new British taxes, but saw them as part of an illegitimate, evil plot to snuff out their rights and freedoms.[1]

People like to think of themselves, and want to be seen, as fair and ethical. Tom wanted to be fair; the union representatives wanted justice. But even though they would eventually settle the contract, they both thought the agreement was unfair and were frustrated and bitter. Justice is a universal value, but people come to very different conclusions about what constitutes justice in specific situations.

Justice is not a simple concept. It needs to be worked out rather than decreed. Tom cannot by himself ensure that the union will accept the contract as fair. Tom and the union people have to reach that conclusion themselves.

It is through the give and take of positive conflict that people come to understand everyone's contributions and needs and accept the rules and how the rules should be applied. Perhaps people do not get all that they had hoped for, but they come to see why the agreement is mutually acceptable and how it satisfies, to a degree, the legitimate concerns of all.

Justice is a result of productive conflict; injustice stimulates conflict. People who believe they have been illegitimately frustrated are angry and in conflict. Employees who believe that their supervisor has treated them harshly for no legitimate reason are angry and file grievances. Union leaders who believe the company's offer is unfair may recommend a strike. A boss reprimands an employee who is inexcusably absent from work.

Injustice can foster conflict that, if well managed, establishes justice. Dealing with grievances and complaints is an important way for organizations to reach out for justice. If, however, injustices are not discussed and dealt with, employees can feel exploited and their rage will be massaged; they may be poised to burst out into destructive, difficult-to-manage conflict.

Overview of Justice Research

A brief overview of research in justice illustrates that by going through positive conflict managers and employees can come to believe that their company is fair and just. While there are some behaviors that are generally unjust, for many issues determining justice is a matter of resolving moral disagreements, not just following a rule.[2]

Distributive Justice.

A primary issue in justice is how the outcomes of group action are shared among the participants. What are the contributions that people are asked to make, and what are the benefits that they derive from being in a group and organization? People contribute ideas, time, energy, and other resources, and in return receive money, status, recognition, affection, and other rewards.

At Lee, people make a variety of contributions. Investors contribute capital, workers use the machinery to make the cement, maintenance keeps the machinery in good repair, the computer group updates the process systems, management oversees and solves problems, and so on. For their contributions, people expect returns. *Distributive justice concerns the rules that guide how the rewards should be dispensed among people and groups.*

There are several popular rules about how rewards should be distributed. One is *equity:* what one receives relative to others should be determined by one's relative contributions. People who give more should get more; high performers should get high rewards. Another rule that is often employed, even by the most conservative of companies, is *equality*. Everyone is entitled to enroll in the health care plan by virtue of their membership in the organization. Individual rights to speak out, to be protected from abuse, and to be valued as a person are shared among all employees, regardless of their contributions.

At times rewards are distributed according to the *needs* of individuals, even in companies that see themselves as highly capitalistic. A company may allow an employee whose spouse has died an extended time off; employees may send their condolences, bring over food, and offer their cabins for a retreat because the person is in need. It is often argued that managers should have higher wages and more flexible hours than workers because their responsibilities are more onerous and therefore their needs for autonomy and relaxation are greater.

Even if people were able to agree on what rules should apply in a specific situation, they would still disagree about how the rules should apply. If they believe equity should determine wages, how can they measure the relative input of the president, middle manager, worker, and janitor? Inevitably, people will be well aware of their own inputs and value them, and less knowledgeable about the contributions of others.

In most situations, people use a combination of equity, equality, need, and other rules. People should be compensated based on the market as well as equity and needs. It appears that employees can find a great variety of situations fair and just. Many companies have developed profit-sharing plans to promote a sense of justice, yet IBM, for example, is widely regarded as a fair employer, but it does not have profit-sharing.

Procedural Justice. The processes and procedures used to make decisions about how rewards should be distributed and punishments handed out are also important justice issues. The workers at Lee are not only concerned about the final contract, they also want to know how the contract is being negotiated. If they believe that management was open and straightforward, they are more likely to conclude that the settlement is just and that the company deserves their commitment.[3] Trust that people are making an effort to be fair, respectful treatment, and the absence of biases are the ingredients that build a sense of justice.[4]

Being involved and having a voice in how issues have been ironed out has repeatedly been found critical to establishing a sense of justice.[5] Indeed, people sometimes value the involvement more than the rewards, even rich rewards.

The value of participation, having a say, underlines the point that people consider a variety of issues and facts as they make judgments about justice. They realize that there are different procedures and rules that could be used and that rules can be applied in many ways. If they are involved, they are apt to understand more clearly the reasoning used to arrive at the solution, to have had their questions addressed, and to have some control and influence over the decision. They will have directly confronted different interests and discussed opposing positions and will understand the rationale behind the decision.

If people are removed from a decision, they tend to second-guess it and suspect its rationale. Uninvolved people are apt to be insensitive to conflicting, legitimate interests and points of view. When workers are uninformed about the financial state of the company and its need to attract investors, they are apt to focus on their own claims for higher wages, not company profits. Uninvolved people often feel that they are unjustly treated, and angrily want compensation.

Few managers doubt the desirability of having a just organization, but many wonder whether it may not be a luxury, given today's realities. Competitive and investor pressures have compelled restructuring, massive layoffs, and other tough actions. Yet companies that appear unjust court disaster. They break a basic human bond that can alienate their work force and lay the groundwork for low commitment and productivity, sabotage, and strikes.

On the other hand, justice does not require companies to shy away from tough decisions or to always give employees what they want. Justice requires that all sides be considered. Justice does not mean general pronouncements and talk about being fair, or that problems are swept under the rug. Justice requires that conflicts be dealt with openly. *Positive conflict is needed to integrate the many and at times opposing claims and ideals if people are to conclude that their organization is just and ethical.*

What Can Be Done?

People, though angry when injustice is done to them, also appreciate that justice is an ideal not always clearly defined nor easily achieved. What is critical then is that the organization be working toward justice, and be seen as honestly attempting to be fair and just.

Positive conflict helps Lee become a more just company. By seeing that the conflicts between production and the computer group, Sara and Rick, Michael and Sheldon, and the union and management are well managed, the people at Lee can conclude that they are fairly treated.

The assumption that the production department was the most important one contributed to its conflicts with the computer group and Sara. Yet all groups are important and must work together to produce high-quality cement in high volume at a reasonable cost. The company teams need to deal with the production department's unjustified sense of superiority.

Lee could take additional steps to make itself a fairer organization and improve how it manages conflict. A complaint-handling and dispute-resolution system would give all employees a legitimate channel through which to identify issues and participate in their resolution. Such a system would explicitly identify the rules of confidentiality, honesty, and fair play which everyone would be expected to follow.

Complaint-Handling Systems

Whistle blowers charge that their organizations have been unethical or unjust in their treatment of the environment, people, and communities, and have covered up misdeeds. They often face ostracism on the job and risk their jobs and careers. Organizations should take a proactive approach by establishing a complaint-handling, dispute-resolution program to which all employees can bring problems they have with their boss and others. In this way, problems can be dealt with before they become disasters, and the company can establish a reputation for fair, ethical behavior.

Lee had an elaborate grievance system in place as part of the contract with its unionized employees, but not with its office and managerial staffs. Lee could draw upon the experience of many companies that have developed complaint systems for all their employees. These companies recognize that they may be embarrassed or even taken to court by employees who charge they have been sexually harassed, passed over for promotions, and in other ways unfairly treated.[6] If a company deals with the problem more directly, the issue can usually can be solved without the costs of public, legal action.

IBM, AT&T, NBC, Security Pacific, Control Data, and many other companies have developed procedures for their employees to express their concerns and get problems resolved. Professional counselors at NBC, employee relations managers at Digital Equipment, and resident managers at IBM help employees voice their concerns and resolve their problems. The ombudsman at AT&T Information Systems, personnel communications directors at Anheuser-Bush, and mediators at Carleton College work to resolve problems through fact finding and mediation. At Control Data, employees have telephone and personal access to professional, personal, and work counselors. They can use a four-step complaint procedure that ends with peer-review committees. A special channel is available for discrimination complaints.

Employee-complaint systems recognize that bosses and employees have difficulties resolving their conflicts directly. Bosses can force their solutions on employees; employees are unsure how they can voice their concerns. Traditional ways of dealing with such problems are limited. Employees fear reprisal if they talk to their boss's boss; they do not want to appear to be disloyal or to be called troublemakers. Employees also doubt that higher-ups will have the motivation and knowledge to do anything about the problem.

Perhaps as many as one-third of all US employers have developed complaint procedures. These systems should be accessible. Employees should have be able to turn to hot lines, managers on the shop floor, and ombudsmen. Attitude surveys and regular meetings with people two levels up also can improve access. The systems should be safe to use, should protect confidentiality, and should forbid reprisals. The system must be credible so that employees believe that their concerns will be taken seriously and that problems will be resolved.

Complaint systems work best when they strengthen the ability of managers and employees to manage their conflicts. They should improve communication, create motivation to deal with employee concerns, and provide assistance to solve problems. Mediators and counselors work to have the manager and employee sit down and discuss the problems. Effective complaint systems help to move companies away from the policy of always backing up the boss, supporting the hierarchy, and viewing dissent as disloyal, and toward appreciating the importance of managing conflict. Successful complaint systems convince managers and employees that the company wants them to discuss and solve problems together to create a just workplace.

Tom and management were trying to change their adversarial relationship with the union. They accepted that they had not kept them informed and had made other mistakes. They wanted a more cooperative labor-management climate. They were beginning to think of some kind of gainsharing program. If they could work with the union to develop it, such a program would contribute to a sense of fairness and partnership between them.

Racism and sexism corrupt organizational life. Rights and the respect of individuals are violated and discriminated against on the basis of race and gender. A program to appreciate these and other differences could have more fully involved all people and been an important avenue for personal and organizational growth.[7]

Concluding Comments

Successful contract negotiations was a goal shared by the management team and the union at Lee. Although they both wanted a settlement that was fair to each side, their difficulty was that each thought the other was unfair. Management felt taken advantage of and the union felt exploited. Underlying the conflict was the belief that justice did not prevail.

Changing this view of an organization is difficult. There is no blueprint that managers can follow that will create a sense of justice. However, managers can encourage it to develop through openness and positive conflict, which demonstrates a respect for the views and rights of others. Complaint-handling systems and gainsharing programs are structured ways to promote a sense of fairness. By these means, employees see clear evidence that the organization is working toward justice.

Justice is an abstract ideal, but it provokes strong feelings. Justice cuts two ways. A just company can reap much commitment and energy because people want to think of the organizations they are part of as just. People who see their organization as unjust do not want to identify with it, and hold back or even sabotage it. People and groups must grapple with issues and voice their opposing ideas and interests to create solutions that they can agree are fair and make them proud of their company.

References

1. D. Tjosvold, "The American Revolutionary Pamphleteers Conservators of Seventeenth Century English Radicalism." Unpublished A.B. Thesis, Princeton University, 1967.

2. T. L. Beauchamp and N. E. Bowie, *Ethical Theory and Business* (Englewood Cliffs, NJ: Prentice-Hall, 1983)

3. G. E. Fryxell and M. E. Gordon, "Workplace justice and job satisfaction as predictors of satisfaction with union and management," *Academy of Management Journal* 32 (1989):851–66.

4. T. Tyler, "The psychology of procedural justice: A test of the group-value model," *Journal of Personality and Social Psychology* 57 (1989): 830–38.

5. J. Greenberg, "A taxonomy of organizational justice theories," *Academy of Management Review* 12 (1987): 9–22. E. A. Lind and T. R. Tyler, *The Social Psychology of Procedural Justice* (New York: Plenum, 1988).

6. M. P. Rowe and M. Baker, "Are you hearing enough employee concerns?" *Harvard Business Review,* January–February (1980): 92–100.

7. D. Tjosvold, *Team Organization: An Enduring Competitive Advantage* (New York: Wiley, 1991).

Part V
Conflict-Positive Organization Development

The conflict-positive model guides the work of managers, employees, and change agents in developing their organization (Chapter 11). The model specifies their common aspirations, and suggests strategies they can take to strengthen their diversity-positive values, cooperative goals, sense of power and confidence, and continuous improvement.

Chapter 12 summarizes the argument that positive conflict contributes very significantly to developing organizations that have competitive advantages to survive and prosper. It is through synergy and teamwork that new products get developed, quality manufacturing is established, and costs are reduced. But managers and employees need a clear understanding of positive conflict and the skills to make these innovations work. Positive conflict is a tough-minded, practical approach to confronting difficult business issues. At the same time, however, positive conflict respects individual's ideas and feelings and is also a soft, people-oriented approach, which is needed to gain high commitment from contemporary employees.

11

Program for Organizational Renewal

Working together in a democratic fashion on a day-to-day basis proved to be the hardest thing most of us had ever done
Patricia Carrigan, Plant Manager, General Motors

Conflict appears in many guises and places in Lee and other organizations. Michael and Sheldon fought over autonomy; the computer group and production department argued about glitches; Sara was angry that operations people did not take her accounting procedures seriously; and Tom was exasperated that the unions found the settlement unfair. These conflicts were carried out in many ways. Sheldon used sarcasm to vent his feelings; production workers stormed and made demands on the computer group; Sara pressed her point and refused to compromise; Tom tried to straighten out the "facts" and the union.

Lee employees used the conflict-positive model to improve how they dealt with their various differences and frustrations. The model was both the end and the means. It was a model of effectiveness that helped them analyze the present situation and agree on where they wanted to go. It was a model of intervention that guided their efforts to become a conflict-positive organization.

Model of Effectiveness

Positive conflict was the framework that Dale, Michael, and others at Lee used to analyze their present situation and decide what they wanted to strive for. This model was critical for their learning how to manage conflict. Tom, Steve, Rick, and Michael—not Dale—had to develop and implement solutions to their conflicts. Dale wanted the employees at Lee to have the ideas and skills to work through present and future conflicts. They needed to understand the model and then work together to implement it.

Diagnosis

As in most negative conflicts, the computer group and the production department were blaming and complaining about each other. The problem was that each thought the other was a villain who was too overbearing to work cooperatively and manage conflict. But this diagnosis itself escalated the conflict as each side felt unfairly treated and insulted, and each sought a measure of revenge. The computer group and production both focused on how the other side should change. *They blamed their problems on the arrogant, irrational ways of the other group, not on how each was contributing to a conflict.*

Competitive, win-lose dynamics of negative conflict were in full stride, and with all the complaining, it may seem that at least people at Lee were confronting the conflict. In fact, though, they mostly practiced avoidance: while they griped to each other and their bosses, they seldom directly discussed their feelings with each other. Only when a crisis was upon them did they talk face to face about the conflict, but in ways that left both sides even more alienated.

Yet the seeds of positive conflict were embedded in the negative conflict. Each group voiced its feelings and grievances; each knew its losses and costs. They had a common goal to make cement, and a need to end their destructive conflict. They had basic communication skills. Their challenge was to draw out these positive-conflict elements and make them dominant.

Common Ideal

Dale wanted Michael, the computer group, the production department, Tom and Steve, the task forces—all Lee employees—to manage conflict. Cooperative conflict would be the predominant mode; it would be the basis upon which they worked. Sometimes people might still try to avoid conflict and even try to win, but important issues would be discussed openly and cooperatively. As they read articles and discussed issues, they came to accept positive conflict as their goal.

Figure 11.1
Positive Conflict

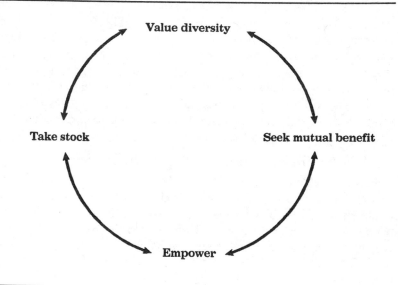

The idea of managing conflict is idealistic and challenging. People must express their views and feelings and listen open-mindedly; they must question accepted solutions and create new ones. Yet *positive conflict is realistic*. It does not ask employees always to be harmonious or to give in and give up; it does not pressure them to be perfect and loving. It recognizes that employees at times make mistakes and fail to understand and respond to the needs of their coworkers. Positive conflict is also practical because it can be directed at relationship conflicts where suspicious attitudes and win-lose ways of managing conflict very much interfere with communication and joint problem solving. Employees at Lee were recognizing that, while they have biases and hostilities, managing conflict was not beyond their capabilities.

Model for Intervention

One learns by doing the thing; for though you think you know it, you have no certainty until you try.
Sophocles

> *Knowing is not enough; we must apply. Willing is not*
> *enough; we must do.*
>   Goethe

An outside consultant or a manager can begin work on any of the components of positive conflict. If employees do not value diversity and avoid discussing issues directly, the change agent can emphasize this need and provide settings for open discussion. Dale worked to have Michael and his computer group see their cooperative goals with each other and with production. Yet, as negative conflict was ingrained at Lee, much effort on all aspects of positive conflict was required over several months.

Value Diversity and Confront Differences

Dale talked about the inevitability of conflict with Lee employees. The goal of the program was not to eliminate differences but to make use of them. He emphasized how Lee needed the diverse skills and perspectives to make cement. He interviewed them on specific times they had dealt with conflict productively. The company was coming to share the value and reach a consensus that diversity is human and constructive.

Open confrontation focused on the contentious issues initiated positive conflict. Through dialogue, Michael and Sheldon clarified the confusions and assumptions that made them suspicious. Sara recognized her style of dealing with disagreement and her anger as she talked with Rick. As Lee employees confronted, they began to understand each other's perspectives and were more prepared to work together to solve their joint problems.

Seek Mutual Benefit and Cooperative Goals

Employees have much latitude in how they consider and frame their goals. The production group can define their objective as getting the computer group to admit its mistakes and follow their directives, or they can see it as learning to work with the computer group to develop a reliable system. The union representatives can see their job as making management look bad and feel guilty by talking about injustice, or as working with management toward justice as a common ideal. Union and management can define their negotiations over wages as competitive: how to make the other give the most so that one's own side gets the most. Or they can define negotiations cooperatively: how to achieve a settlement that keeps both workers and management committed to working together to make the plant productive and a good place to work with secure jobs.

Production and the computer groups talked about the importance of their common goal of developing a reliable system that made cement. The production people could be confident the system would work and that glitches would be solved expeditiously. The computer group would earn respect and would avoid being called out to the plant in the middle of the night to troubleshoot.

Empower

The computer group was dejected because, despite their best efforts to improve the system, the production department was still upset. The production department was frustrated because, though they stormed and banged, the computer group was still distant. As in other negative-relationship conflicts, they doubted their own abilities as well as mistrusted the intentions of others. They felt powerless as their own individual attempts to resolve the conflict failed.

A major objective of the conflict program was that the people at Lee should feel that they, not their conflicts, were in charge. They took relatively small steps to deal with tough conflicts. Dale worked with Michael and then the computer group for some time before they met with Rick, Greg, and Loren. After the meeting, they reflected on their successes and honestly assessed how they needed to improve. They were seeing that while there was no easy solution, together they could move forward.

Confrontation meetings, task forces, and other formal settings supplemented informal communication in the hallways and coffee room. Rick, Glen, Loren, and Michael established biweekly meetings to discuss frustrations, develop new projects, and avoid crisis management.

The people at Lee, as in many other organizations, had little formal training in positive conflict, though they had developed skills (and bad habits) through a lifetime of conflict. Michael and the computer group practiced handling confrontations skillfully and appropriately and learned to dig into the issues. They avoided surprises, insults, and confusions, and listened and put themselves in the shoes of production.

Taking Stock

In the negative conflicts at Lee, there were the seeds of positive conflict. But similarly, negative conflict can emerge and replace productive conflict. People can stop discussing issues and frustrations, begin to think in win-lose terms, and feel distrustful and apathetic all over again.

Regularly reflecting on conflict managing and thinking about how to take small steps to get better is the way to maintain and strengthen the momentum and improve their abilities. The first session of the computer group with Rick, Greg, and Loren was not perfect, but it was a beginning and one that they learned from.

The Consultant's Role

Not the cry, but the flight of the wild duck, leads the flock to fly and follow.
        Chinese proverb

Positive conflict guided Dale's relationship with Steve, Tom, Michael, and others at Lee. Dale had a different perspective and on occasion would have opposing ideas. But he confronted these differences openly, emphasized the shared aspirations of making Lee conflict-positive, integrated their ideas and interests into an effective program, and met with Steve and others to discuss progress.

Value Diversity and Confront Differences

As he wanted people at Lee to recognize and value their differences, Dale was open about his differences with them. Because of his background, he was convinced that conflict, if well managed, had great value. Michael and others had read articles and discussed these ideas, so they understood his perspective. Employees at Lee often thought that avoiding conflict was acceptable if not ideal. Dale argued that avoidance could be the most damaging of all approaches to conflict.

The people at Lee tended to see their conflicts in a win-lose, "I'm-right-and-the-others-are-wrong" way. Dale pointed out how he saw both parties contributing to the conflict, and how both could and should benefit from its resolution. Michael thought that Sheldon was a troublemaker he had reason to suspect; Dale argued that Sheldon's openness could be a real asset for Michael.

Seek Mutual Benefit and Cooperative Goals

These opposing points of view did not mean that Dale's goals were opposed to those of Lee's employees. His interests and theirs were highly compatible: his goal was to create an effective program that would help Lee manage its conflicts to facilitate productivity and morale. Dale told employees, "I'm working for Tom, Steve, Michael, Rick, and you." He was not to trying to make one side win, or even to make Steve and Tom win, but to make everyone win.

Positive conflict served as a common goal for Dale and Lee employees. Dale questioned Michael's approach to getting a new computer system on the basis that it was not a positive-conflict approach. Because Michael had already accepted the value of positive conflict, he did not consider Dale's feedback gratuitous and arbitrary and instead realized that it pointed out how his approach fell short of a common ideal.

Empower

Dale argued that the people at Lee could be in charge of their conflicts, not controlled by them. However, he did not have the answer and could not by himself empower them. They had to work with him and each other to develop the attitudes and skills to manage their conflict. Dale demonstrated the basic conflict-management skills of listening and communicating for Lee to model. But he reminded them that managing conflict was difficult and that neither he nor they could always be expected to handle themselves perfectly.

Taking Stock

Dale met periodically with Michael, Steve, and others to get feedback on the program and his behavior to learn early of dissatisfactions and misunderstandings. He tried to be open-minded and to avoid time pressures and crises. Discussions with Steve helped to enlarge the program so that it became organization-wide.

Managers as Change Agents

Steve, Tom, and Michael contributed to making Lee more conflict-positive. They recognized the need for conflict management, were open to Dale's ideas and suggestions, and worked with him. With or without an outside consultant, leaders have an important role in managing conflict. They work for diversity and confrontation, mutual benefit, and an empowered work force.

Steve and Michael were beginning to show that they *valued diversity*. They recognized the diverse skills and perspectives in their organization, and talked about how that contributed to its success. They backed up talk with careful listening to different points of view, and by demonstrating that they had heard. They respected and enjoyed the differences in personality, background, ethnic membership, training, and outlook. They revealed their own positions, but in ways that encouraged others to speak out.

Steve and Michael wanted to *focus the organization on cooperative goals*. They talked about "our" goals and "our" accomplishments. They showed how everyone benefits when the group succeeds. They praised and provided incentives for joint success. They held themselves and others responsible for failure. They managed conflicts to get mutually advantageous agreements.

They *empowered*. They reminded employees of their common goals and mission and that they could, by working together, overcome barriers. They provided opportunities and encouraged the development of skills. They involved employees through task forces. They invited Dale to develop sessions where the Lee employees could discuss issues and refine their skills. They worked for *ongoing improvement and celebrated* when conflicts were productive.

How Realistic Are Cooperative Goals?

Some researchers have argued that, especially for important issues, organizational members are in competition and must engage in political activities to win the conflict.[1] Our studies suggest that cooperative goals are quite common. Unfortunately, there is insufficient evidence to estimate the frequency of cooperative and competitive interests.

An important aspect of organizational life that makes cooperative goals feasible is that employees must work together over a period of time. They seldom have just one conflict, but need to collaborate in the future and work out additional conflicts. To the extent that they focus on the long-term, they are apt to conclude that their goals are cooperative. If they try to win and alienate the other, they realize that future collaboration will be more difficult. If they are reasonable and work for mutual interests, it is more likely that others will be helpful in the future.

Two people in competition for the same promotion do not necessarily have to fight competitively. They can understand that they are going to have to work with each other after the promotion. They can see that it is in their mutual interest to restrict the competition to fair rules. They must continue to work together and help each other do their jobs to demonstrate their fairness and responsibility. A "no-holds-barred" competitive struggle could undermine both their reputations and futures.

How about those conflicts that have escalated and already inflicted damage? Competitive, escalating conflict induces people to focus on the short term, differences and incompatibilities, winning and not losing. Yet, even here, adversaries can begin to reframe the conflict as cooperative. They have the overlapping goals of reducing the conflict and anger, controlling the costs, and ending their common misery.

Intervening in a Highly Conflict-Negative Organization

Though it had considerable negative conflict, Lee had definite strengths upon which to build a conflict-positive organization. Their devastating strike five years ago had left many with vivid experiences of a conflict that escalates uncontrollably. Steve and Tom had decided that they wanted to do something about the conflicts within Lee. In addition, people like Rick were very open with their feelings and did not pretend they weren't in conflict. Rick, Michael, and others were honest, decent people without psychological pathologies.

Some organizations, like West Cement, the corporate office of Lee, are more conflict-negative. Because of restructuring and mobility, there were few people at West Cement who remembered the strike; the few who did were not close to the havoc it wreaked on people's lives. The corporate head office had the common goal of making the company profitable and attractive to investors, but this goal was not was as concrete and measurable as making cement.

The climate at West Cement was political and competitive: factions were in quiet warfare. They distrusted each other and defined many issues as undiscussable. Confrontations were avoided; people used indirect ways to pursue their agendas over those of others. They were intelligent, verbal, and well trained, but not skilled in relationships. They had developed elaborate defenses ("We are tough-nosed businesspeople who do not need touchy-feely ways of working") and strategies ("I'm too busy and too important to find the time to deal with minor issues like people's hostility and anger") to avoid conflict. They were pessimistic and dismissed conflict programs as idealistic.

A positive-conflict program is possible, though far from easy, even in such a climate. A major stumbling block is that people do not want to admit and own up to their conflicts. They fear facing up to how ineffective and dishonest their relationships are. Getting people to sponsor such a program and discuss their frustrations openly can be very difficult. However, such conflict-negative organizations have elements, though deeply buried, of positive conflict. Indeed, people are often losing a great deal and, if they believe that a conflict program can be successful, can be highly motivated.

Concluding Comments

The conflict-positive model helped the computer group, production, managers, and Dale together strengthen their organization. Through reading and discussing they came to see that they had a *shared conviction* to develop positive conflict and make it work for them. They also acquired a *common knowledge base* about what constituted effective relationships and conflict management. They *worked together* to strengthen their valuing diversity, seeking mutual benefit and believing their interests were cooperative, enabling each other to deal with conflicts and get the job done, and reflecting upon and developing their abilities. They also made efforts to extend positive conflict and work for *continuous improvement.*

Work at Lee is far from over. Inevitably, there are lapses into the negative conflict of avoiding, fighting, and blaming. Michael forgets to lead *with* his team, and Sheldon and Glenda feel out of touch and uninvolved. The computer group barks back at the production employees rather than appreciating their dilemmas and digging into their problems. Task-team members dismiss minority views; Steve closed-mindedly sticks to his original position.

Lee employees must continually strive to manage conflict. They have momentum, but old habits and attitudes can move them back into negative conflict. Even well-managed conflict has rough edges as people argue, fight, state their grievances; it is easy to feel self-righteous and suspicious. *Becoming a conflict-positive organization is a journey, not a destination.*

The conflict-positive model is a powerful guide to dealing with the great range of conflicts in organizations. It is straightforward, but not simple-minded. It does not offer a quick fix. Negative, competitive conflicts and the attempt to avoid conflict grow out of the culture and structure of organizations. They are usually a sign of a range of shortcomings and problems that will not be made right by a simple technique or by following two steps. Positive conflict provides an elegant way to examine many aspects of organizational life. It is an integrated approach to changing organizations, that, if used wisely, transforms and revitalizes them.

References

1. J. Pfeffer, *Power in Organizations* (Boston: Pitman, 1981).

12

Positive Conflict as Competitive Advantage

By blending the breath of the sun and the shade, true harmony comes into the world.
Tao Te Ching

The nineties, according to General Electric Chairman Jack Welch, "will be the white-knuckle decade for global business...fast...exhilarating." The competitive international marketplace is not a slogan, but a reality.

Because each company has unique circumstances, strengths, and weaknesses, it must devise its own way to respond to changes and develop competitive advantages.[1] There are no blueprints or simple formulas that a company can use to survive and prosper. But positive conflict can help people understand demands and pressures and develop the direction and organization necessary to create value and serve customers.

Experimenting with flatter structures and employee involvement, fostering synergy among new product engineers, shop floor workers, and marketing personnel, and exploiting new markets through joint ventures require positive conflict to capture competitive advantages. Yet these changes pose barriers to managing conflict. People are asked to work together who do not know each other well, have little experience and practice in dealing with their conflicts, and are trained to think in much different ways.

When production at Lee was computerized to cut costs drastically, Rick was asked to learn the language and purposes of computers, and to work with Michael. They had very different backgrounds, lifestyles, training, and values. It took time to learn to understand each other and trust that they could manage their conflicts openly and cooperatively. As international joint ventures become more common and the work force becomes increasingly diverse, employees will need to be particularly skillful and sensitive to manage conflicts with people whose backgrounds and outlooks are very different.

In a slower-paced world that tolerated slack resources and inefficiencies, people could take time to develop relationships, let procedures emerge piecemeal, and use trial and error to learn how to manage their differences. Today's pressures make these strategies obsolete. *Contemporary managers and employees must have a clear understanding of positive conflict and its procedures and skills to make innovations work.*

Reconciling Organizational Dilemmas

Positive conflict, I have argued, reconciles the views and interests of divisions and people into workable solutions that promote common aspirations. The conflict-positive perspective also reconciles long-standing dilemmas of organizational life. Managers and researchers have traditionally thought that organizations could either promote the collective good or individuality, emphasize either productivity or people, and be either tough-minded or soft-hearted. Breaking away from these assumed trade-offs helps create organizations that achieve competitive advantages.

The Collective Good and Individuality

Organizational issues are often framed in terms of the individual versus the organization. Do the requirements for corporate action take precedence over the needs of individuals? Where do employee rights end and their responsibilities begin? When does a company have the right to suppress the rights of individuals? Japan and other Asian countries are thought to emphasize the collective good at the expense of the individual. Though there are at times trade-offs, positive conflict asserts that collective and individual goods move together.[2]

Individuality is needed to breathe life and energy into a group and organization. The right of individuals to speak freely, to be respected and valued, and to voice their own interests and aspirations contributes very substantially to realizing the common good. It is through such individuality that the collective discovers where to go and how it is going to get there and creates the unity to get there.

A positive-conflict organization fosters individual expression. People realize that their individuality need not be self-centered, but is valued by others. Team players are not replaceable parts of a machine, but vital, unique people and contributors.

People and Productivity

Managers have been told that they should to the extent possible promote people as well as productivity.[3] They should strive to enhance their people so they have the energy and commitment to pursue organizational goals. Yet many managers see productivity and people as an "either-or" choice.

Positive conflict provides a way for managers to be compassionate about people and passionate about productivity. Employees who can manage their conflicts are energized and empowered. They identify more with others as they learn their feelings; they develop their thinking by incorporating the ideas and reasoning of others. They feel a sense of genuine support that reduces stress. They get feedback, know how others see them, and become more self-aware. Through conflict, Michael learned and appreciated Rick's values and openness, and thought less rigidly about workers and unions.

Positive conflict has clear benefits for the organization. Information is shared, issues are discussed, and effective decisions are made. Employees exchange their resources and use their abilities to help each other accomplish their jobs. With positive conflict, there is a great deal of synergy between promoting people and productivity.

Tough-Minded and Soft-Hearted

Managers traditionally think of hard and soft approaches to managing and changing organizations. "Soft" organization development has been criticized as based too much on the ideology of participation, the value of trust, and the need to treat people gently and as being too removed from the reality of power.[4]

Conflict-positive is a both a tough-minded and a tender-hearted way to manage and change organizations. People at Lee were to trust and be sensitive to each other's needs and styles, and to become involved and work together. Yet they were also expected to confront. They revealed their frustrations, asserted their demands, and questioned each other's positions.

Steve and Michael were asked to be conflict-positive managers. Steve was to be supportive and broad-minded, but he was also expected to challenge conclusions honestly. He would certainly not just hand over his authority to company teams, or be tolerant, or "let the people decide." He would remain involved and powerful. Michael was to work with his team, but he was still very much the architect and central player within the computer group.

Confronting Challenges

You never conquer the mountain. You only conquer yourself.
Jim Whittaker, First American to climb Mt. Everest

You can't do it alone.
Don Bennett, Seattle businessman and amputee, when asked his most important lesson from climbing 14,400-foot Mt. Rainier

A dilemma remains: if conflict is so pervasive and valuable for competitive advantages, why does it conjure up so much negativity, and why have so many managers and employees created conflict-negative organizations? People and companies seem to put much more energy into avoiding conflict than making use of it.

The conflict-positive perspective, as we have seen, challenges traditional notions of organizing and managing. It is intellectually demanding to understand the implications, requires effort and risk taking to develop skills, and asks us to be open to varied feelings and expressing them.

Important barriers, such as the pervasive emphasis on the short-term, frustrate an organization's efforts to become more conflict-positive. People want to get through the day and complete the immediate job quickly. Dealing with conflict and creating a conflict-positive organization are long-term strategies that some people never get to.

The habitual thinking that every conflict is a fight to be won or lost gets very much in the way. People equate conflict with destruction and havoc and assume that they must avoid it until they feel pushed into a corner. The myth of the individual interferes.

Many managers and employees want to solve issues by themselves. They want to be the hero who rides in and saves the day. Leaders assume that they are supposed to take charge and resolve conflicts unilaterally. As we have seen many times at Lee, *managing conflict requires mutual work.*

The hold of these worn-out attitudes and myths is strong. Many people are highly invested in the ways they have developed to deal with conflict. Asking them to change raises objections and fears. Under the stress and pressure of conflict, they fall back to well-known habits. Education and training, unfortunately, often add to resistance. Schools and universities promote a competitive orientation in which students are asked to show up, outdo, and get better scores than their classmates.[5] Management education has emphasized technical knowledge and skills and undervalued skills in working with others. Many educated, senior managers are highly committed to proving that they are right and others wrong.[6] They have learned through education and experience the wrong lesson.

Yet, as the people at Lee and many other organizations attest, positive conflict is an attainable goal. They are developing climates and forums in which they can deal honestly and directly with their differences. Even in poorly run companies, employees, we have found, are able to manage at least some of their conflicts well.

Though it challenges some traditional ideas, positive conflict very much builds on basic values of honesty and open-mindedness and it is forward-looking and personal. Managing conflict is a very human, everyday activity.

Companies confront ongoing change and uncertainty. They need to be poised to appreciate emerging opportunities, circumvent pitfalls and threats, and realize competitive advantages. Through positive conflict, managers and employees take the long-term view, anticipate and exploit changes, and keep in touch with each other as well as customers, suppliers, specialists, and investors. Positive conflict is a fundamental competitive advantage for it helps organizations develop strategies to position themselves to growing markets, and create, manufacture, and market high-quality products.

References

1. C. C. Lundberg, "On organizational learning: Implications and opportunities for explaining organizational development." In R. W. Woodman and W. A. Pasmore (Eds.), *Research in Organizational Change and Development, Vol 3* (Greenwich, CT: JAI Press, 1989), pp. 61–82. R. W. Woodman, "Organization change and development: New areas for inquiry and action," *Journal of Management* 15 (1989): 205–28.

2. D. Tjosvold, "Rights and responsibilities of dissent: Cooperative conflict," *The Employee Responsibilities and Rights Journal* (in press).

3. R. R. Blake, J. S. Mouton, and A. A. McCanse, *Change by Design* (Reading, MA: Addison-Wesley, 1989). M. Sashkin and W. W. Burke, "Organization development in the nineteen-eighties," *Journal of Management* 13 (1987): 393–417.

4. W. R. Nord, "OD's unfulfilled visions: Some lessons from economics." In R. W. Woodman and W. A. Pasmore (Eds.), *Research in Organizational Change and Development, Vol 3* (Greenwich, CT: JAI Press, 1989), pp. 39–60. M. Sashkin and W. W. Burke, "Organization development in the nineteen-eighties," *Journal of Management* 13 (1987): 393–417.

5. D. W. Johnson and R. T. Johnson, *Leading the Cooperative School* (Edina, MN: Interaction Book Company, 1989).

6. C. Argyris and D. Schon, *Organizational Learning* (Reading, MA: Addison-Wesley, 1978).